One Man, One Voice

PARTHIAN BOOKS

One Man, One Voice

Plays by

Mark Jenkins
Ed Thomas
Ian Rowlands
Roger Williams
Frank Vickery

Edited by

David Adams

PARTHIAN BOOKS

Parthian Books
53 Colum Road
Cardiff
CF10 3EF
www.parthianbooks.co.uk

First published in 2001.
All rights reserved.
© Parthian Books
ISBN 1-902638-09-3

Typeset in Galliard by NW.
Printed and bound by ColourBooks, Dublin.
With support from the Parthian Collective.

The publishers would like to thank the Arts Council of
Wales for support in the publication of this book.

Cover: Josh Richards in Playing Burton
©Guy Masterton

A CIP catalogue record for this book is available from
the British Library.

Foreword

Definitions

David Adams

Titles are important because they are always calculated. *Playing Burton, Envy, Marriage of Convenience, Saturday Night Forever, Sleeping with Mickey*: all are pregnant with meaning - albeit often an ironic one. And so with this volume, although it is one chosen by the publisher rather than me, *One Man, One Voice*.

Let us define our terms, then. I quote the dictionary:

One: single; only.
Man: a human; an adult male.
Voice: sound produced by the vocal organs; that which expresses a message or meaning; expressed opinion; an invisible guiding or directing spirit; the right to have a part or share in the deciding of something; verb form indicating relation between subject and verb.

In our *One Man, One Voice* this is not the Man of pre-feminism's mankind. And indeed, because each of these monologues (or to be more precise, monodramas) does represent one man's voice there is a companion, *One Woman, One Voice* that acknowledges, if we need to, that a voice has a gender. Discourse is not neutral or asexual and maleness is certainly one of the most important defining characteristics, if not the most important; more perhaps than colour, class or culture. The male voice usually speaks of power, of domination. Interestingly, one contributor, Roger Williams, writes for a gay character, and another, Frank Vickery, for a female, which could lead us into more consideration of gender.

So all these voices are male; they are also Welsh - insofar as each playwright has some claim to be Welsh, though only three are Welsh-speaking. The Welshness I mention at the outset not so much because this volume is a Welsh product (a Welsh publisher backed by Arts Council of Wales money) but because it informs the voice: the one writer who might not want to be corralled into Welshness, Mark Jenkins, speaks through the familiar voice of a famous Welshman, Richard Burton. The others have a Welsh rhythm and often a Welsh vocabulary and in two cases *(Envy* and *Marriage of Convenience)* overtly offer a debate about Wales and Welshness. I note this from the edge, being non-Welsh.

A voice is more than language. According to dictionary definition, it embodies message and meaning; it can also mean an expressed opinion, suggest a right to be heard, even suggest a higher, spiritual authority; and we use it in grammar (nominative, accusative and so on). Talk about a voice and we have to consider modes of address, articulacy and questions of subject and object. I promise not to get too academic, but we have to think, perhaps, of the distinction that has obsessed modern thought, between signifiers and signified, about subjectivity and identity, about representation, about difference, about the slipperiness of meaning as regards the word. The monodrama, crucially, relies virtually entirely on one channel of communication, the voice: no other "signs of performance"[1] in this semiotic discourse, no action, no proxemics, no other characters, little gesture, usually minimal sets and costumes. Just the voice. One voice. One man's voice.

One man's voice: an individual, unique, even isolated voice. The monologue can be, well, onanistic; it can be paranoid. After all, what is a monologue but someone speaking to themself? A lot, actually: it is a device to speak very directly to lots of people, an audience, and one that will not answer back or engage in dialogue. While we sometimes feel that a monologue is a private musing we overhear, it can also be something shared, wherein we become complicit, especially in the form of a monodrama. There is also the notion that the character delivering the dramatic monologue is a bit like the Ancient Mariner, someone who's buttonholed you. But the singularity of the monologue means that issues like identity and individuality, the ego, superego and id, are present, whether stated or silent.[2]

Every narrator creates voices. Aristotle and Plato identified three basic kinds of narration - the narrator's own voice, the assumed voice of someone else and a mixture of their own voice and others. T S Eliot also defined three positions (though talking about poetry) - the voice of the writer talking to themselves or to nobody, the voice of the writer addressing an audience, large or small, and the voice of the writer creating a dramatic character. The question we avoid is which of these voices we are hearing.

Should we be concerned? Does the author matter? What is "real" or "authentic"? Is "verisimilitude" the nearest we can get?[3] In each of these five monodramas a writer has created a persona (persona is the Greek for mask, let us not forget), a "false" voice. The reading of these, however, can be complicated by the realisation that in no other dramatic form is imagination so tied to (auto)biography as it is in the monodrama.

Richard Burton was, of course, a real person, though no longer able to prevent Mark Jenkins from putting words into his mouth. Jenkins offers us his version of the actor Richard Burton and has given him words to say which, the author might presumably argue, explore with creative freedom Burton's perceived personality. Although, of course, "Burton" is not the real Burton but the invention of Mark Jenkins and accordingly says what the author wants him to say. Despite this we, in this age of the "death of the author", feel able to listen to the character as a voice in his own right and neither the original real person nor the mere puppet of his creator.

Edward Thomas's anti-hero in *Envy*, Ted John, is also, by

Thomas's own admission, based on a real person although of the five people we meet in these pages he is the nearest to a created character even if his story is based on actual residents of an actual place (and is peppered with presumably actual incidents retold in Thomas's other plays). Ted is a truly fictional character, a man who is seen to have such a distorted view of reality that it makes him behave in an abnormal way.

But Alex in Ian Rowlands's *Marriage of Convenience* is also to some extent "real" - he seems to represent the author, and reappears in Rowlands's *Blue Heron in the Womb* and *New South Wales* - Alex is Rowlands's alter ego. We infer that Rowlands speaks through Alex and of the five characters this is the most seemingly autobiographical; to an extent Alex is real because we believe him to be (rightly or wrongly) the author and he has an authenticity because of this.[4]

It is tempting to see Roger Williams not only as sensitive Lee, the narrator in *Saturday Night Forever*, but also as the extrovert Matthew, and the two as facets of the same authorial character: one a sensitive introvert, the other the extravagant extrovert (though neither is exactly deep, it may be that the third character, intellectual non-camp Carl, represents another part of the author). But while as a composite, he/they may represent aspects of the author's personality, they nevertheless retain their own identity.

On the surface only Frank Vickery's immensely sympathetic creation Eileen in *Sleeping with Mickey* is removed from its creator - she is, after all, a mature lonely mother. We cannot but feel, however, that there is a good deal of real-life drama and suffering in her fictional story: she is obviously not the author but she certainly is recognisable and has "verisimilitude".

Burton, Ted John, Alex, Lee and Eileen are five people trying to make sense of the world - or rather each is a character created by their author as his way of trying to make sense of the world, and their monodramas are the means by which their creators share with us this project.

So in these five plays, just who is saying what to whom, how are they saying it - and why?

Footnotes appear at the end of the book.

Mark Jenkins was born in North London to Irish/Welsh parents. He has worked as a musician, soldier, journalist and lecturer in economics. He moved to Cardiff in 1980 to take up a post at the University of Glamorgan. His first play, *Birthmarks*, won the Drama Association of Wales competition in 1986. It has played in Cardiff, London and Stuttgart. His second play, *Playing Burton*, opened in 1992 and, including two sell out seasons at the Edinburgh Festival, has been running almost continuously since.

Other work includes *Strindberg Knew My Father* (1992) published by Aurora-Metro, *Downtown Paradise* (1996) & *Mr Owen's Millennium* (1997). He has also worked successfully in television and film. *The Scarlet Tunic*, adapted from a Thomas Hardy short story premiered at the Odeon, Leicester Square in 1998. He is currently working on *Tiger Bay*, a film about the boxer Jim Driscoll and *Atonement*, a film adaption of his play *Downtown Paradise*. Mark claims never to have had a bad review or a first production in Wales.

Playing Burton

Mark Jenkins

First performed at the Etcetera Theatre, Camden, Autumn 1992
Producer - David Bidmead
Richard Burton - **Josh Richards**
Director - **Hugh Thomas**
Running time: 85 minutes

Second production at The Edinburgh Assembly Rooms as part of
the Edinburgh festival, August 1994.
Producer - Masterson Productions
Richard Burton - **Josh Richards**
Director - **Guy Masterson**

During radio announcement of his death, Burton walks onstage and sits smoking, and reading from the Complete Works of Shakespeare... As announcement fades (to the mention of Under Milk Wood) he rises...

BURTON

It was all going to happen for me, and I knew it... But not why.
I was aware that my people had nothing, yet I wanted for nothing.
It seemed like providence... But I did not know.
I was filled with wonder; a sense of destiny which trampled over circumstance, as if to some purpose... Death robbed me of my mother's love, yet I was loved to death by all my sisters. Oh, I was spoilt with love!
I lost two sisters on the way... So... still... like undivined jewels trapped in cold black stone. I could have been one of them. They perished, I did not.
When my brothers were hungry, they set food before me on the table. They laboured in darkness while I stretched my arms up to the sunlight.

And what is the purpose of it all? Why should I be Richard; wear the crown? No one has ever been able to explain that to me.
And what is this 'talent' I possess...? Some call it... 'a gift'. I find that unsatisfactory. Why give to one and not another?

What is it they say about a gift? That it's the thought that counts..?
The thought... Or lack of it! If there is anything at all behind creation it is not 'thought', or love, morality or meaning, and surely not... benevolence - a kind of arbitrary force which scatters love, pain, joy, death... 'gifts' at will... An endless, random game of dice.
Good and evil become two sides of the same confusion.

I feel a great stillness within me - People say it shows on stage - Yes... a stillness...
Why me play Richard? If there is a God then he was drunk at my conception, just like my father...drunk, too, for most of his eternity!

So, you see, I wanted... Need... to be closer to what made me who I am.

...And, at last... *for a few brief shining moments,* I felt as though appearances were falling away, and I could reclaim myself for myself.

He sits

I wanted desperately to play Lear for two or three years, but my neck was broken, and you can't play Lear in that condition...

The King has to lift a young woman in his arms - difficult, with a perforated ulcer and one's entire spinal column coated with crystallised alcohol... They had to open me up and scrape it all off with a scalpel...

Lear is a Welshman - 'Llyr' in Welsh. The word 'England' is never mentioned in the play. Lear is King of Britain. Shakespeare is writing about pre-Anglo-Saxon Britain. He deliberately mangles the language. It's wrought, and taut, and strangled.
Some of the lines are unspeakable, but they have to be said. It's as if Shakespeare's tearing himself apart.
It would be nice to play him in the English theatre... but I find English theatre so boring these days... Broadway is infinitely more exciting: You can open a show at eight p.m. and by one o'clock in the morning you know whether to catch the next flight out because it's dead, cut, finished.
But at the Royal Shakespeare you can play for a whole season with bad notices, people will still come... Why? Because it's the Royal.

I don't find that interesting. I think you should have to fight the way Edmund Kean had to fight; David Garrick had to fight; Henry Irving... Did I fight?

In Lear's own kingdom they speak the language of Heaven, the language I was brought up in. My parents in the chapel spoke the language of King Llyr and I'm bilingual to this day. At home with friends sometimes I surprise an English guest by slipping into it... It isn't for effect. It's me. It's us.

I can remember... I must have been eight or nine... one day reading a poem in an old yellowing book with pages falling out. It was under the heading 'English Literature'... and I could feel the strength and beauty of this foreign tongue... All that I have done, I have done in a language that was not my own.

He rises

'My mother died when I was two. My eldest sister Cis took her place and brought me up with her... Now my sister was no ordinary woman - no woman ever is, but to me, my sister less than any. When my mother had died, she, my sister, had become my mother and more mother to me than any mother could ever have been. I was immensely proud of her. I shone in the reflection of her green-eyed, black-haired, gypsy beauty. She sang at her work in a voice so pure that the local men said she had a bell in every tooth and was gifted by God... She had a throat that should have been coloured with down like a small bird, and eyes so hazel-green and open that, to preserve them from too much knowledge of evil, should have been hooded and vultured and not, as they were, terrible in their vulnerability. She was innocent and guileless and infinitely protectable. She was naive to the point of saintliness, and wept a lot at the misery of others. She felt all tragedies except her own.'

I had read of the knights of chivalry and I knew that I had a bounden duty to protect her above all other creatures. It wasn't until thirty years later, when I saw her in another woman, that I realised that I had been searching for her all my life.

'Now as I was young and easy,
Under the apple boughs,
About the lilting house,
And happy as the grass was green,
The night above the dingle starry,
Time let me... play...'

I had a Welsh accent you could cut with a knife. However, I was fourteen and left school early to help Cis with my beer and cigarettes.

He sits

Know what my ambition was?
To squat on my haunches on a Saturday street-corner with the ankles of my trousers bound with string; my blue scarred miner's arms folded 'cross my chest to show the mark of a man; chewing on a match stick to impress the girls... and whistling as they passed, half a crown in my pocket to swill the coal-dust from my belly... Oh my horizons were... lower than the horizon.

I could have been buried alive with my boyhood boyos, digging themselves deeper into the darkness until their bodies turned to coal, unadored in their brief and gentle manliness.
How many Burton baritones have gone unsung, above them the earth? And that's what I thought I wanted...to be below with them.

In the meantime I settled for the worst of all worlds...

He rises

I took a job in the 'gentlemen's outfitters' department of the coop store.... Haberdashery.... Shabby...

One morning I was cleaning brass on the shop door when along came my old teacher, Meredith Jones... Now, you didn't mess with Meredith Jones...

Mornin.

- What do you think you're doin', Jenkins? -

What do you think I'm doin? I'm cleaning the bastard brass!

He clipped me round the ear and told me not to speak with a cigarette in my mouth.

But I've left school now, Misser Jones

- No you haven't. You're just about to start... immediately... understand?

It was the hardest thing I'd ever done in my life. A drop-out going back to school. No! Even harder were those voice sessions with Philip Burton... every evening until ten, eleven, twelve o'clock....in the 'room of terror'.

- Now how seriously do you want to be an actor Jenkins?

Very serious, Mr. 'Bearton'... I've never been more serious... I'll work... I'll work harder... harder than I've ever done... I know I can do it!

But that time I first read Hamlet for him...

- Here Jenkins, read this...

'Tobe or Noddwbe; thaad is the qweschan

Wheatha tis norbla in the maend to suffer

The slings an' arroz of aoutrajus forchewn

Or to take aarms against a seee of trubble...'

- Kindly pause for a moment Jenkins, I think I need a large sherry.

Do you laek it Misser Beart'n?

- I used to Jenkins... I used to like it... Tell me... do you know what the words mean?

Oh aye... I mean, yes, Misser Bearton.

- Then tell me what the prince is thinking in this piece...

I think the Prince... is in two minds... I think he's trying to work out what to do with his life... whether to... 'take arms against a sea

of troubles'... the obstacles that confront him... 'and... and by opposing, end them'... change his situation for the better... instead of dithering, you know... take hold of things...
Master his own destiny...

There was a long pause. He looked at me fondly... put his hand on my shoulder and said... 'Well done, Richard. Now I think we can start.'

Wild Jenks at seventeen – boxing poet with a magic uncle, salvaged from six months of living hell in haberdashery, from a cul-de-sac of long johns! Wild Jenks – closet ciggy smoker in a vanishing playground; boozy scholar, boy of many parts, peeing from train windows as we rattle through a platform of spellbound passengers - my first public appearance in Wales!
I have a wild ambition to go out into the world and starve for something beautiful... become a preacher: I'd show you sin in a posy of primroses... and redemption in a barmaid's thighs; innocence in an old man's laughter, and true companionship in a good, clean scrap. I'd recreate the world in seven words with a few... well-tuned... silences.

I am in love with vowels. Knocked out by consonants, I believe they were made for each other and I was made for them. I want to dwell with them forever on dusty coal-tips, along the charmed embankments of the railways and on the viaducts of heaven.

I want to be the authentic voice of the Valley of The Shadow of Coal; the deep, dark voice of real men, whose life is work and who deserve no less than hold the centre of the stage.

No!... I'll play for Wales! Win a cap! Don the Red Jersey! Do battle with the English enemy... 'Yes, here he comes, the new cap from Pontryhdyfen... along the touch line dummies one man... two men... He's going for the gap! He's over! Superb in its creation. This young man who only last week won the Welsh

Youth light middleweight championship is faced with a difficult choice... rugby, boxing, poetry, preacher or Prime Minister!'

He sits

Yes... There's a lot you don't know about me. Even more I don't know about myself.

Do you remember when you were a kid with the evening sun at your back and the rest of time before you... and from your feet there sprouts forth this... colossal shadow of yourself. And every tiny step bestrides a mountainside.
You're like a puppet master with a giant hanging densely from your strings, yet light as air! One finger raised becomes a gesture of the infinite and the sky is silence. You can take it... take it all!

One day my shadow just... cut loose and bounded off across an ocean and a continent... and left that little kid with empty strings. A boy without a shadow.
Yes if he wanted to follow me Little Jenks would have to change his name, give up the language of his birth, trade in his father and hide himself behind a mask, take on a thousand parts within a labyrinth of words... Lose himself to find himself.

Philip Burton taught me to use English like a sword - not that mincing nanny-goat 'Oxford English' in which 'man' and 'men' dissolve away to 'meahn'. All consonants were liberated like 'as-k-ed' and 'dep-th-s' - and this enriched the vowels. It was emancipation. What he revealed I grew to love and I became my teacher's son. I moved in with him and took his name. He was committed to me... and all he ever did he did for love of me.

Oxford! - It took a world war and the RAF to get me in. It's like a foreign country. Full of Fellows... all airs and graces... but not above borrowing money off me.

'By Jove - you've played Emlyn Williams on the West End stage? I say... you couldn't lend me a fiver, could you?'

Neville Coghill makes me understudy for the part of 'Angelo'. I can miss drill and grow my hair long. One day, Angelo vanishes in a puff of smoke... nervous breakdown or something... Poor fellow. West End impresario Binky Beaumont comes to see *me* in performance... loves me! 'You absolutely must come to see me in London, darling, when this beastly war is over.'... So when the beastly war is over, darlings, I do... and he signs me up immediately. Ten pounds a week... A fortune.

How does a Prince become a King? I spend the war discussing these strategic matters with Robert Hardy and Warren Mitchell in local pubs, between rugby matches...

Now... Take the two parts of Henry the Fourth and Henry the Fifth as one piece... Prince Hal is all three. As separate plays the prince is overshadowed by Hotspur in part one, by Falstaff in part two, but lo and behold the wretched boy becomes King in the last play.... But see it as a whole. See the Prince as apprentice... Now you've got three very different plays: Hal working his way from back street pubs... Harry making his way to the throne; Henry ready to take on the world... The perfect part.

And... after working for Binky Beaumont and landing a film contract... it happens, and I'm ready to take on Stratford - where, according to Kenneth Tynan I bring on my own cathedral with me... where I am also 'spotted' by Humphrey Bogart and Lauren Bacall who duly report back to the powers that be in jolly old Hollywood... and then...

He rises

Cry God for Richard, Broadway and... DARRYL F. ZANUCK!

I'm loaned to Mr Zanuck... I have no say in it... He stars me in

'My Cousin Rachel' and 'The Robe'. They do so well he insists he has me under contract... and then he sues me.

On one side of the courtroom - Darryl Zanuck and half the corporation boys in America. On the other side, me, alone - no lawyer. I play it very English, very Ronald Coleman:
Suddenly, one of the lawyers jumps up, shakes his fist at me. -'You shook hands with Mr Zanuck on this agreement. You shook hands with Mr Zanuck in his own office.'
I reply, 'I don't believe Mr Zanuck said that because Mr Zanuck is an honourable man. But if he did say it, then he's a fucking liar.'
The place breaks up in confusion. Strong men faint and are carried off by weak men.
The next morning, the telephone rings... there's a woman on the end of it. 'Did you call Darryl Zanuck a fucking liar?'
'Yes, I think I did.'
'Then you need help, I'll be right around.'... She becomes my first legal adviser. It's now a very different world.

He sits and pours a drink

My first party at a swank house in the Bel Air district of Los Angeles. Sunbathing by the pool - Kirk Douglas and Hedy Lamar - drinking highballs, iced beer... long wet brown arms reach out of the pool, shake my paw. 'Hi there Dick!'
'Don't call me Dick,' I say, '...makes me feel like some kind of symbol.'
I am enjoying this small social triumph when a girl sitting on the other side of the pool, lowers her book, takes off her sunglasses and looks at me with such... coolness... a new ice cube forms in my Scotch & Soda.
She is so extraordinarily beautiful I nearly laugh out loud - a combination of plenitude, frugality, abundance, tightness...
She sips some beer, goes back to her book... and she is totally ignoring me... not interested in talking... not yet... Not for some time yet.

He lights a cigarette

'Well, take this of me, Kate of my consolation
Hearing thy mildness praised in every town
Thy virtues spoke of and thy beauty sounded
Yet not so deeply as to thee belongs,
Myself am moved to woo thee for my wife.
And will you, nil you, I will marry you...

Now Kate, I am a husband for your turn;
For, by this light whereby I see thy beauty,
Thy beauty doth make me like thee well,
Thou must be married to no man but me...'

He approaches a director's chair marked 'JENKINS'

Jenks... it's time you and I had a serious chat... You're growing up and there are a few things you ought to know... I'm married - or hadn't you noticed? Her name's Sybil. I love her. You'd love her too... She's one of us, same blood, same side of the tracks. Her hair is silver... She's like a mother to me...
But Jenks... I can't leave girls alone... She knows, I think... she understands.

He rises

Well, look, we're surrounded by limp-wrists in this game. It's no job for men...traipsing around in make up and tights. Don't get me wrong, some of my best friends are Queens... really high camp Royalty! But 'Oh the women come and go talking of Michaelangelo.' I've steered a path through galaxies of stars and starlets. If they were up and coming, so was I. In shrubberies, shower-rooms, walk-in wardrobes... I came out once wearing the husband's suit! The question is, Jenks... Why do I do it?

Now there are people called psychologists... And they say that obsessive womanising is symptomatic of latent homosexuality - yes Jenks, one of those! It may be true, but if it is, isn't it uncomfortably close to the reasoning of O'Brien in *Nineteen Eighteen Four*? Is freedom slavery? Is black just latent white? Was Einstein merely a latent subway mugger... you know, had a bad start in life... got into trouble with the laws of Physics?

Psychologists complicate life - perhaps people with inferiority complexes are just plainly inferior... nothing complex. We have to believe in free will... we have no choice.
You're a lucky boy... We're both bloody lucky... And there's more than one brief shining moment on the road from Prince to King... To King... of Camelot!

Telephone rings

Hello, King Arthur speaking... Joseph Mankiewicz?... Cleopatra? In Rome? With Who?! How much? Plus villa and expenses? You'll have to talk to my agent... you'll have to buy me out of Camelot - never Welsh on a deal. It's called chivalry, love ...Arrivederci!

'What will be, shall be. Divinity, Adieu!
Aye. There are those that Faustus most desires. Oh what a world of profit and delight, of power, of honour, of omnipotence is promised to the... movie star!
Shall I make the spirits fetch me what I please?'

Addressing bottle and pouring

'Great Mephistopheles! - One thing, good servant, let me crave of thee,
to glut the longing of my heart's desire,
That I may have unto my paramour
That heavenly Helen which I saw of late,
Whose sweet embraces may extinguish clear
Those thoughts that do dissuade me from my vow

And keep the vow I made to... Lucifer...!'

....Oh Marlowe bach!

He drinks

I wonder what she'll be like - that vision from the poolside in Bel Air?

He pours

'As to her person, it beggared all description: She did lie in her pavilion - cloth-of-gold a tissue - o'er-picturing that Venus where we see the fancy outwork nature. Age cannot whither her, nor custom stale her infinite variety: other women cloy the appetites they feed; but she makes hungry where most she satisfies: for vilest things become themselves in her, that holy priests bless her when she is riggish.'

He drinks

It took a long time ... but at last she was talking to me.

Telephone rings

No, this is Mark Antony's butler. He's busy... Cunnilingus, you understand... Cunnilingus - you invented it - Well, you are Latin aren't you?... It means... an Irish air hostess! Ciao!

Puts phone down - Phone rings:

No, this is the Vatican... I'm having dinner with God...

Desk? How much are they paying to put these phone calls through? ...Well I'll double it... family and business only, got it!

Puts phone down - Phone rings:

Jesus Christ speaking... Oh! Philip!... Sorry... No, I haven't been drinking. Yes, I got your cable... Philip, I know you're fond of Sybil ...so am I... Listen Philip, I'm thirty seven years old... Act like it? Now stop being an interfering old auntie... Philip!... Philip!... Damn!

Puts phone down - Phone rings

David Lloyd George speaking... Ifor! Ifor, thank God... I've just had Philip on the line... Eddie Fisher's having a breakdown... Elizabeth's been rushed to hospital... food poisoning supposedly... Sybil's upset?... that's all you care about? But Ifor... don't hang up... Ifor... Et tu Brute ...

Puts phone down

Dwi am briodi'r 'eneth 'ma... I will marry her...

Dials Telephone

Jack!... Jack, look, I know you're in charge of publicity but this is ridiculous... My fault? Jack, love... how was I to know she'd knock Krushchev off the front page?.. I know we're making a movie... Listen, love, why don't you just wind up Cleopatra and get the camera crews into my bedroom... Just me in my breastplate and Miss Tits... Much cheaper, and authentic... Well, it's cost three million already and art hasn't caught up with life yet... Elizabeth and I are way ahead of you. No we're not acting on set - it's for real... She wants to marry me... Why not?... I'm married, that's why not!... Yes, I have denied it... so I denied the denial... should I deny that I denied the denial?...

Aside, to the audience:

It's the most public adultery in the history of the world...

Continues on telephone

...Cameramen, journalists, paparazzi! I don't care if the Vatican does condemn the film, it's my life at stake here... No, no, no, divorce is out of the question. I've got two kids and Sybil... Yes, I love them all... So, your money's on Elizabeth... Bye, Jack!

Slams phone

Dwi am briodir 'eneth 'ma. I *will* marry her.

Telephone rings

Elizabeth? Elizabeth!... Elizabeth? Oh, well, the ring of the telephone... sounded different.... Listen... Rwyn dy garu di! Mwy na neb arall yn y byd!

What does it mean? It means ... '*Sweet Helen, make me immortal with a kiss. Your lips suck forth my soul: see where it flies. Come, Helen, come, give me my soul again. Here I will dwell, for heaven is in those lips, and all is dross that is not Helena.*'

... Faustus!...Faustus, oh never mind! Look, I'll be right round... I've got to see you.

So, I've won! ...and lost everything. I owe so much to Sybil and we're both so desperately worried about our little Jessica... She'll probably never speak. The doctors say a trauma...

But, I have to be with Elizabeth. It's more potent than will, resolve or duty. Sometimes two people are like stars in each other's orbit.

And she blazes through my life like a daily Halley's Comet, trailing sparks of celestial debris... You should see the bathroom... a massive fallout... bras, slips, stockings, talc, perfume... the place is radioactive. She knows the world will go round picking things up after her.... but she fusses over me... brings me cooked lunch on set, makes me eat my greens, arranges my hair... laughs at my stories. She's even drinking beer and watching rugby... just wants to be the tidy wife... so it's love alright.

...She's been called a 'chorus girl', a 'scarlet woman'. It can't be easy... and the Jenkins's of Pontrhydyfen... their loyalties aren't easily transferred and we're a pretty overpowering clan. Well, wait till they hear I've stopped chasing... stopped wanting other women, or rather wait till they get around to believing it.

He rises

I'm on the monogamy wagon! In Camelot the chorus used to sing... 'I wonder who the King is screwing tonight!'... But now, I've met my match.

Who is it she reminds me of? The eyes, the bearing and the presence... After this 'I say there will be no more marriages'...

And in the darkness of a thousand drab suburban cinemas... people pay to share our off-screen passion. We are the universal edition of every married partner's secret fling... A yearning that recedes before them like a half-remembered dream... and we get paid for it! Get married on the proceeds...

After Cleopatra some of the scripts we're sent are diabolical. My opinion of them is even lower than critics.

I mean the most incredible things happen in Hollywood, even before breakfast. Incredible. It's real-life surrealism! In Hollywood they really do believe that Salvador Dali was just a lucky photographer. You know, he just happened to be there when those watches were melting.

Now, there was this guy, a producer - now, I swear to you this is true - and he knocked at my door one morning with two armfuls of film from the cutting room floor. He says... 'Say, I've just made this movie, and I've got all this stuff left over... Seems a pity to waste it... Look!' And he ran it through his fingers against the light.

And it was all shots of army vehicles and personnel... in the desert... Second World War. 'Who's that?' I asked. He took the cigar from his mouth. 'Oh that's George Peppard... but at a distance, it could be you.'

And so we made this movie, oh... in a couple of weeks. He bought in some writers to write short scenes in between all the long shots from the trash can. I played George Peppard close-up and he played me long distance... and nobody knew the difference. We put it on release and it did okay. Not big bucks, but it made money and I had fun doing it...

Garbage - literally - all expenses paid.

Box office six: Art nil.

When I was a kid, I used to sell horse manure at tuppence a bucket. Thirty years later it was fetching millions! Now there's inflation for you!

To salve my conscience I play Hamlet on Broadway. Hamlet without women's clothing. Hamlet, American style like a rehearsal. Hamlet to standing ovations and rave notices. Hamlet, a record one hundred and thirty six performances. A six million dollar Hamlet - a million of it mine... More than I made in Cleopatra and three other movies put together.

Then, at Oxford I really did sell out to the Devil... as Doctor Faustus. I knew that would please the literati. I fluffed my lines as Helen of Troy knocked back Bloody Marys in the wings...

The Randolph Hotel never recovered from the shock. The critics enjoyed a week of vitriolic sadism; all the money went to charity and everybody had a wonderful time. The school prefects were vindicated... Elizabeth and I shot off to Rome...

He sits

So here we are, the old story... Boy meets girl... Just the two of us... and the secretaries... and the secretaries' secretaries; our private photographer; one valet each; a make-up artist; tutors for the kids, a governess, oh, and a nanny. Then there's the financial advisers, two accountants and a bodyguard... We even have to exercise the dogs on the roof in case they're dog-napped - which would break Elizabeth's heart...

And outside, in the corridor, there's a man with a machine-gun to stop anyone with another machine-gun bursting in to take us all prisoners.

Picks up some letters

Yes, quite a large retinue really. You see, we have to preserve our privacy even if it means sacrificing our privacy.

Bob?... Where is he?... Bob? - Oh, Bob's my right hand man. Protects me from unwanted phone-calls... If you want to get a message to anyone here, you have to put it in a bottle and just hope it reaches dry land... Bob!... I get a tidal wave of correspondence. Who's this? ...Good God... Tim. We served in the RAF together... he was winger... I was flanker... Did we reply to this letter from Henley? Bob!

He rises

Do you know, I wish I could just... walk out of here to a quiet bar across the street and have a beer and a chat - not a hope! Cleopatra fans everywhere, thousands of them, screaming their heads off. We have to be spirited out of side doors, fire escapes... into laundry vans and police wagons. If I wanted to burgle this joint I'd know six different ways of getting in.

Dials telephone

Engaged! It's always bloody engaged.

Taps phone

Hello desk? Can I have a line out please? ...Well, alright, you get me Mr Robert Hardy... Robert Hardy... H.A.R.D.Y... No, not Russell Harty... Oh, forget it!
Well, I tried...

Some force, some need, some thing elemental. As if a loss had been restored... I can't explain. She and I... It had to be.

Picks up Complete Works of Shakespeare and reads:

'Blow winds and crack your cheeks! Rage! Blow!
You cataracts and hurricanoes, spout
Till you have drenched our steeples, drowned the cocks.
You sulphurous and thought-executing fires,
Vaunt-couriers to oak-cleaving thunderbolts,
Singe my white head! And then, all-shaking thunder,
Smite flat the thick rotundity o' the world!
Hmmmnn!'

A rare privilege... my own obituaries. Rave notices? Not on your life. Even in death the critics descend on you... to judge the final performance...

He sits

and I can tell you I'm destined for a poor exit.

'The Times'... 'Began his career as a performer of fine promise on the classical stage. This made it seem that he was destined for the commanding heights of the profession... in spite of occasional forays into the cin-e-ma.'

'How now? Mend your speech a little lest it may mar your fortunes!'

'Virginia Woolf was powerful in purely cinematic terms.'
Well, it was a bloody film!

'After 1947 he devoted himself to his stage career and to... the pursuit of young women who apparently found him irresistible.'

...'Apparently!' An envious thrust, methinks, from one who lacks in penetration... Ah, listen to this. What does Johnny say...

'He was a born actor but he was a little bit wild, and chose a rather mad way of throwing away his theatre career.' - What an old... sweetie! 'He was cursed with enormous... sex appeal... He had only to turn those large blue eyes and every woman was smitten.'

'*When I do stare, see how the subject quakes! I pardon that man's life. What was thy cause? Adultery? Thou shalt not die; die* for *adultery? No...*'

'Summoned by the Sirens of Hollywood.' - 'A Prince who abdicated.' - 'Immense promise not fulfilled.' - 'In Sir John Gielgud's controversial production of Hamlet, Burton was... tensely exciting and moving' - I say, steady on - 'but apparently visibly flawed.'

Why 'apparently'? - Quite simple... The chap who wrote this didn't see it. 'Visibly flawed' and he didn't even see it! - Now there's perception for you!

...The English critics can forgive you flouting tradition... Hamlet in blue jeans... And they can understand rave notices... in America...

He adopts an 'English' accent

'The Yanks are short on self control - long on razzmatazz - I'm sorry to say... a mongrel breed...' - A hundred and thirty six performances on Broadway... you'll get away with that... But... to make a million as the Prince of Denmark... A million! Just not cricket old chap.

Far more edifying to play Hamlet... in tights... in London... for peanuts... and submit yourself to ritual thrashings by the Times, the tax man and the master race.

He sinks to his knees slowly

Then you can creep out of a lonely stage door, purged of arrogant pride, chastened by the literati, drown your sorrows in half a pint of bitter, and beg forgiveness from Art... from England... and from the Test and County Cricket Board....

He sits

Flagellation - the English bloody love it... They do it for the pain.

'The bastard Philip Faulconbridge in King John was a role he fitted exactly...' - 'The most nominated actor never to win an Oscar.' - 'Where did Burton go wrong? Perhaps nowhere...' - Come on now boys, you're not trying... 'He never came even close!'...

'They durst not do it. They could not, would not do it... Tis worse than murder to do upon respect such violent outrage... How sharper than a serpent's tooth it is to have a thankless child!'

...'Burton colluded in the myth that he was a great actor' - The Guardian ... 'The myth'?

'Oh I will do such things - what they are yet I know not, but they shall be the terrors of the earth!...' You'll answer to my Lear for that. I'll give you bloody Leer!

He rises

'Doth any here know me? This is not Lear. Doth Lear walk thus?
Speak thus? Where are his eyes?
Who is it can tell me who I am...?'

I am a descendant of King Llyr. I'm Welsh... And in those far off forgotten realms I was one of thirteen... Some died... With a father, no mother, and we lived on a dollar a week! Five shillings. A penny per day, per person... We had to steal sheep from the blasted heath... pretend we'd found them dead... That was our welfare!

Never even came close!

'Oh let me not be mad, not mad, sweet heaven
Keep me in temper. I would not be mad!'

James Joyce once wrote in a Belle Letre or something... that every man is searching for the place he belongs to...
I've always believed that... that I would turn the bend in a road and suddenly be home...
Well, I never made it - I was denied it.
Perhaps it's not a place at all.

Perhaps I'm still looking for Ritchie Jenkins.

So you see, I'm more than ready for the King in flowing robes, shaking locks... His world of storms and incredible events... His verbal music, melancholic poetry - where only fools and lunatics speak sense, and a father holds his young dead daughter in his arms... and the victim is still nobler than the forces which destroy him... Yes, I'm ready for that.

'... *Spit fire; spout rain*
Nor rain wind fire are my daughters.
I tax not you, you elements with unkindness.
I never gave you kingdom, called you child.
You owe me no subscription...'

He sits

Yes, I'm ready for Lear now... but not a Shakespeare audience. Have you ever looked at a Shakespeare audience? I don't mean to be unkind - but have you? All those middle-aged ladies who regard it the way Catholics regard confession... a penance for not having sinned with real conviction... and they drag their golfing husbands along with them... and the poor fellows sit there horror-stricken - with eyes like liquorice allsorts... and it dawns on them that they did all this at school as a punishment, looking at their watches to see when the interval is due. Personally, I'd like to introduce positive vetting for Shakespeare audiences... Yes, the audience should be limited to, say, two hundred who weren't frightened by Shakespeare in their cot.

Well I've blown the knighthood... Out of the window...
Play Shakespeare in England - it has to be England, not Broadway - do it long enough, they make you one of the cast... a member of the court... but in the USA it means nothing. Mind you a lot of Americans do call me 'Sir Richard'... How very democratic - to be knighted by your fans. Even Philip Burton's been knighted over there. I really do believe that Americans are the most generous people on the Earth. Enormously, extravagantly, funnily generous.

I was walking down Forty-fifth street in New York one day, and this little powerfully built American guy stopped in front of me and embraced the whole sidewalk - the pavement - with his arms and said ...

'Dick - God damn it, Dick - you are the greatest God-damn
Macbeth me and the little woman have ever seen... you are the
greatest God-damn Macbeth that ever lived!' And he went on and
on telling me what a great Macbeth he thought I was...
Enormously generous.
Surprising... as I've never actually played Macbeth...
I think he might have seen me in Henry the Fifth.
Hmmmm.

As I said, my first experience with the English language was that
poem I found in the old yellowing book of English literature with
the pages falling out. It wasn't until I was nearly twenty that I
discovered it was written by a Scotsman...

'Unto the ded goes all estates,
Princes, Prelates and Protestates -
Baith rich and poor of all degree,
Timor Mortis conturbat me.'

He rises

'He has ta'en rule oe'r Aberdeen
And gentle rule of Corstophin
Twa better fellows did no man see
Timor Mortis Conturbat me

Sen he, he's all my brether taen
He will nacht lat me lif alane
On forse I man this next pray be
Timor Mortis Conturbat me

... And I thought it was English...'

He sits

I recited those lines of William Dunbar to Dylan Thomas one day. We were... having a drink. Well, more than one drink, actually. You see, Dylan never knew when to stop, and I... I didn't want to. What do you think? I asked him... There was a hushed silence. He slowly lit up a cigarette and said...

- 'Wonderful stuff, marvellous! When did I write it?'

Oh, four hundred years ago - your Scotch period.

- 'Four hundred years? Then it's about time we had another.'

Make it a double! And we did, many times over.

Dunbar didn't exactly put the verses in that order and I changed a few words... You might say that it's a lie... It is... But... the sheer majesty of the words... If Dunbar didn't write it that way he bloody well should have.

What is a lie anyway? Isn't theatre just the noble art of deception - One glorious, enormous, hoodwinking lie... And what does the God of Theatre care for the truth? Why, everything... Lies owe their very being to the truth. Somewhere in the bosom of a bawdy, brazen and Byzantine lie, lies the reason why it's told. Besides... lies are more interesting.

Now when the Welsh tell lies, we really mean it. What happened last week is unpredictable and today we invent yesterday. We must be true to our lie. Deliver it with a passion; fashion its coils and let these colonise the galaxy of conscious being. There must be the lie, the whole lie, and nothing but the lie.

He rises

Now, my old grandfather - now, this is the truth. He used to get about Pontrhydyfen by wheelchair... and Pontrhydyfen is hardly wheelchair country... It was Derby Day and Gran'f'thr had backed the winner - a horse called 'Black Sambo' - so he thought he'd celebrate... get drunk. So, my father wheeled him down to the village pub, pulling on the chair to stop Gramps getting to the bar first.

Well, vast quantities were sunk that night and they left early progressing in good voice back up the hill - which had grown steeper with each pint. At the top, my father sees the front gate... no mean feat in his condition... and with simple, but defective logic, lets go of the chair to open it... He turns round... no grandfather. No indeed. Grandfather is half-way back to the pub at ever-gathering speed, backwards; receding to infinity shouting 'Come on Black Sambo! Come on Black Sambo! Come on boy...'

At the bottom... was a solid, stone wall....

You wouldn't have recognised him.

Light years set me apart from my father's underworld.

You'd think that after losing grandfather, Dick Bach, my father, might have taken the pledge... never touched a drop again. Not a bit of it. I can recall him now, swaying in the doorway of our clean, bare kitchen. Looking with drunken benevolence at his large family. We'd all been warned by my brother Ifor to look helpless, pitiful, reproachable, or downright bloody nasty... but the great smile, the twinkling black eyes, the unforgettable voice... were hard to resist. He'd slept the night in a chicken coup - we could see the feathers in his hair.

Some say social conditions drive a man to drink... But Dick Bach did it because he liked it...

.... I have an image in my mind. It is of a man perched on top of a wall. If he drops down on one side, he's made the last choice he will ever make. He denies himself all other options. He takes his place in an ordered, puritanical Utopia. No risks, no unforeseen eventualities.

On the other side, lies an uncertain world, where he is free to squander his talents or succeed... but most of all... to generally make a fool of himself.

The man is poised on this wall not knowing which side to settle for. One side would be so mind-bendingly, predictably dull it would surely drive him to drink. But in the wild excitement of the other, he'd freely choose to drink himself to death. Alec Leamass - bent on self-destruction - gripped by almost cosmic ... boredom.

'What the hell do you think spies are? Moral philosophers measuring everything they do against the word of God, or Karl Marx? Well, they're not. They're just a bunch of seedy, squalid bastards like me. Little men, drunkards, queers, hen-pecked husbands; civil servants playing Cowboys & Indians to brighten their rotten little lives. You think they sit like monks in a cell, in London, balancing right against wrong?

Yesterday, I'd have killed Mundt because I thought him evil and my enemy, but not today... today he's evil and my friend... London needs him... They need him so that the great moronic masses you admire so much can sleep soundly in their flea-bitten beds again; they need him for the safety of ordinary, crummy people like you and me...'

He gets up

After films like that it's nice to get back to Pontrhydyfen, and sanity. One occasion I drove down there in my new Rolls...

I met Sam the Drop. His aim in life was to be a public hangman. It was the first time I'd spotted Sam outside a pub during opening hours...

He was looking at the Rolls and I asked him if he wanted a lift. He climbed into the back, sank into the upholstery, testing... the strength of the hand strap with neck-snapping jerks...

'No', he said, with a faraway look of nooses, hoods and trap doors, 'I'll just sit yere and enjoy myself.'

Will Dai crossed over to us hands in pockets, cap pulled well down.
- 'Well... if it isn't b..b..bloody D..D..Douglas... F..F..Fairbanks 'imself!'
His stutter had always been bad...
Hello Will... How are things, then?
- 'T..T..Terrible m'n! I jus' l..l..lost s..s..seventy-f..five th..thousand

p..p..pounds.'

How come?

- 'W..Well, I had s..s..seven draws on the f..f..football pools and j..jus' one team l..l..let me down...'

Which team, Will?

- 'Fuh..Fuh..Fuh..'

Fulham? - I prompted him.

- 'N..n..no m'n... Fuh..Fuh..Fuh...'

Falkirk

- 'N..N..no, no... Fuh..Fuh..Fuhking Swansea!'

Yes... It's nice to get back to sanity.

Addressing the bottle:

'Ah Faustus, now hast thou but one bare hour to live and then thou must be damned perpetually.'

He pours... and swirls glass

'Stand still you ever moving stars of heaven, that time may cease and midnight never come.'

He drinks and sits

In penthouse suites at the Dorchester I get up to watch the dawn coming up over London... Always first up. Elizabeth, the children, and the man with the machine gun, all in dreamland.

He pours

For me, dreaming is an effort these days... I can do whatever I like without anyone asking me what I'm doing or why... Ah... *What infinite heart's ease must kings neglect that private men enjoy...*

He drinks

I've hired the most expensive floating dog-kennel the world has ever seen. A thousand a week - to stop a Chihuahua getting lonely in L.A.

He pours and swirls glass

'Oh lente, lente currite noctis equi. The stars move still, time runs, the clock will strike. The devil will come and Faustus must be damned.'

He drinks....
He rises and pours

Let's drink...to the superfluous...

He pours
The useless...

He pours

The extravagant

He pours ... He drinks... He pours...

Diamonds for breakfast... care to join us? Elizabeth beat me at Ping-Pong.

He picks up box with enormous diamond ring and shows it to a female member of the audience.

Herr Krupp's finest, thirty-three carat... five thousand bucks for a backhand volley... ten thousand for a clean ace. Final score... one million - love. Well, I wasn't playing my best...

Slipping down the world's Ping-Pong ratings... It's Elizabeth they pay to see... always notches up bigger earnings than I do. Well, let's drink to Venus de Milo... with or without ice?

He drinks and pours

'The Devil will come and Faustus must be damned.'

He drinks

'Oh I'll leap up to my God! Who pulls me down? See...'

He pours slowly

'See where Christ's blood streams in the firmament; one drop would save my soul, nay, half a drop. Ah, my Christ!'

He drinks

...I've got a present... now, this really is something.

He picks up another even larger diamond and shows it to the same female member of the audience.

Her own private ice rink. The Cartier diamond. Sixty-nine point four two per cent carat. I know she doesn't need it... But my God, I need to give it.
Oh, and these...

He shows off a lovely string of pearls.

The King of Spain once gave these very pearls to Bloody Mary herself...

He puts them on his head like a ridiculous tiara, picks up the bottle and glass... and begins to recite...

'*Oh I know a bank where the wild thyme blows...*' and a yacht with a pool and a cocktail lounge and an organ as big as an oil refinery... We can hire an organist to play Bach when there's a storm at sea... Toccata and Fugue in sea minor.

He pours slowly

'*And see where God stretcheth out his arm and bends his ireful brows. Mountains and hills, come, come and fall on me, and hide me from the heavy wrath of God.*'

He drinks and meanders, and stops up facing the back of the theatre...

Where the hell is everybody? All these gems of the poetic imagination going to waste... I NEED AN AUDIENCE!

He begins to recite again, loudly.

'*You stars that reigned at my nativity,*
Whose influence hath allotted death and hell,
Now draw up Faustus like a foggy mist
Into the entrails of yon labouring cloud
That when you vomit forth into the air
My limbs may issue from your smoky mouths,
So that my soul may but ascend to heaven.'

Know what we'll ascend to heaven on?

He pours

Our own fur-lined passenger twin jet...

He drinks and sits

...Each day it gets harder and harder to scale new heights of vulgarity... all our Van Goghs, Monets, Modiglianis... they offend my social... socialist sensib... sensibil..ities.

He pours

Elizabeth was born to all this... she can cope. Van Gogh, Monet, Modigliani... artists of integrity... I mean... you'd never catch Van Gogh playing the lead in 'Where Eagles Dare' now would you? ... Creates a bad impression... Mind you, he'd have given his left ear for that kind of fee...

Holds bottle to his ear

'This is Vincent calling Danny Boy... Vincent calling Danny Boy.' Why do you think I give so much of it away?

He drinks

...Elizabeth's worried that her arms are getting fat... Know what I say... if thine right arm offend thee, knock it off... That's what Venus did...

...One day I'm going to turn my back on all this. I'm going to be an... honorar... an honorary fellow, Oxford University... at St Peter's... Dreaming spires... a don... take classes in literature...

Addressing the bottle

Oh, '*Impose some end to my incessant pain. Let Faustus live in hell a thousand years. A hundred thousand, and at last be saved. Oh, no end is limited to damned souls.*
Why... wert thou not a creature wanting soul?'

...Last night, Elizabeth broke a whole service of dinner plates over my head... Was it something I said?

...We each create the partner we deserve... not many people know that.

'Oh why is this immortal that thou hast?'

Addressing the bottle

Ah, Pythagoras metempsychosis, were that true. 'This soul should fly from me and I be changed unto some brutish beast...'

He pours

How's the rest of it go?

'...All beasts are happy, for when they die Their souls are soon dissolved into elements... But mine must live and still be plagued in hell.'

He staggers

It's her birthday... We'll fly in five square feet of caviar, fill the bath with Moet and Chandon 1923 and you can all dive in naked... Come on in!... It's lovely once you're in! I've invited the Royal family... They can tell us jokes...
Oh Jesus, I feel awful... what's the matter with me?

He collapses flat on his back, staring at the ceiling

'Look not... so fierce on me... Adders, serpents, let me breathe awhile... and .... and ....'

Well, haven't you realised... I've dried... forgot my lines... just like I did at Oxford.

He leans up on his elbow

I keep on ribbing Elizabeth that she's never learnt anything by heart. She said 'I do know a poem...' Come on then you fat Jewish tart, tell everyone... And she recites the only poem she's ever learned... It went...

'...*What'll you have? the waiter said, as he stood there picking his nose. Two hard boiled eggs, you son of a bitch. You can't stick your fingers in those!*'

He staggers to his feet

Richard's himself again!

'*Let's see now... What else can we do?... There are other games we can play. We've played 'Humiliate the Host'... we've gone through the one, haven't we... How about... How about... 'Hump the Hostess'... Yes, how about that..? Or shall we save that one for later?... You know, mount her like a god damn dog!... Oh, you don't want to play 'Hump the Hostess'. No... You don't want to play that one... not yet... I know what we'll play... I know... We'll play 'Get the Guests!' How about a little game of 'Get the Guests'? ...*' Who *is* afraid of Virginia Woolf?

He finds his chair and sits down

... Are we Richard and Elizabeth playing George and Martha? Or are we... My God, can it be... Are we George and Martha playing Richard and Elizabeth? The lines remember me; the play interprets us. Well... you know... nothing can survive a play about itself... I mean, actors cannot act themselves... It's like imitating reflections in a mirror, impersonating shadows...

It's hard to tell you this Martha... I mean, Elizabeth... While you were out... making your last movie... the doorbell rang... it was a telegram... from Mr Albee. It was for us. I can hardly bring myself to say it... I'm afraid our marriage won't be coming to its own anniversary party... No... Our marriage can't make it that day... You see, it had been drinking rather heavily, and wrapped itself round a tree whilst trying to avoid middle age... So it's... Goodbye Elizabeth, at least... for now... Oh God...

He staggers to his feet

Uuuunhhhhaaarrrghh... I play Richard... You hear me father?... I play Richard... I wear the crown... The crown is mine, my own... I'm drunk like you... Is the madness in me too? Oh god, is the taint in me too father..?

God I feel awful. What's the matter with me?

Look I... I'm shaking... I'm pouring with sweat... Can it be... Can it be that ... after forty-eight years I'm finally having a hangover? How many did I have...? My usual - three... my head's spinning... three bottles? ...Never made me feel like this before... Must be the cigarettes... I must cut down... to fifty... Oh, this is intolerable... I'm not putting up with it! Those stupid doctors at St John's...

He sits down

Two weeks they've given me... two weeks... Look, It's not that I'm afraid of death... I just can't be killed off this easily... I'm from Welsh mining stock... They promised to come to my funeral... Two weeks drinking time left? Ding-ding... Last Orders...
They say they don't think they can save me even if I stop right now...

He empties the bottle into the glass

Well, doctors love to play God.... Damn them!

He drinks it all

'I dreamed there was an Emperor Antony: O such another sleep. that I might see but such another man! His face was as the heavens; and therein stuck a sun and moon, which kept their course and lighted the

48

little O, the Earth...
Think you there was, or might be, such a man as this I dreamed of?'

The glass slips from his hand to the floor.

He picks it up and reaches for the phone.

Hello... Could you get me St John's Clinic, Santa Monica... It's urgent... Thank you.

He gets up

... Four days off drink... It was bad... very bad.

Always the same... I would dream of my brother Ifor who'd died four years earlier... Ifor was like a father to me... Kind, gentle, strong... never spared me frankness... I would dream he was with me in the room...

It was the Autumn of 1968 the accident happened. I suddenly had this urge to take my daughter Kate to Switzerland to see our new house - 'Pays de Galles'. I took her to lunch... Ifor went ahead to heat the place... When we got to coffee there was still no sign of him... Two hours had passed... So, finally, we went up to the house... It was a... nightmare...

Ifor was lying in the snow... His neck was broken... He was barely alive... He'd been there two whole hours... Slipped on a snow-grill. I tried... I tried... to lift him. Shouldn't have... Damn drink...

We got him to Geneva... intensive care... Gwen and Elizabeth flew straight out... At sixty-one, Ifor was paralysed from the neck down...

There were moments when he didn't want to live and, sometimes... after visiting him or Jessica... I felt the same... *'His life was gentle, and the elements so mixed in him that Nature might stand up and say to all the world - this was a man!'*

He sits

I got back to work... that was something... Played Churchill. Well, if an Irish potato farmer called Harris can play Cromwell, I'm pretty sure a Welsh miner's son ought to manage Churchill...

But as I played Churchill, I began to see him afresh and hate him anew. I began to see him for the vindictive toy-soldier he really was and realised that I hated him and all his kind... I wrote something to that effect in a newspaper and all bloody hell broke loose...

Lifelong friends turned their backs on me. I was slated in *The Times*. Some... man called 'Norman Tebbit' was particularly nasty. I don't know why I did it... Churchill always liked my work. We'd never clashed on a personal level. No, it was something deeper... Something deep rooted from the past...

Yes... quite a difficult time really... all the heroes of my life dying around me... the doctors warning me I could be next... and so, the inevitable happened... One day, Elizabeth and I found ourselves on two ends of the same telephone line... and the temptation to meet up again was irresistible...

I think it was Karl Marx who said 'History repeats itself but the second time as farce.' - And so, on the banks of a muddy river in Botswana, we were married for the second time, watched by one bewildered hippopotamus. It was to be 'for lovely always'... and 'lovely always' lasted seven weeks...
... Of course I was back on this stuff... on and off...

He shows the empty bottle to the audience then places it under the table

...until I met Susan... snowbound on the slopes above Gstaad... trying... trying to comprehend what I'd done.... what I never believed I could...

Swirling earthbound in a halo of frozen sunlight, Susan's smile could put an avalanche into reverse gear.

Susan, my saviour, delivered me from my late Elizabethan period... the dregs of empty vodka bottles, dog-ends and the acrid smell of matrimonial blitzkrieg.

Susan, put me on the stage again... my Equus was a galloping success. Broadway stomped its feet for 'Nogood-Boyo' and his phantom horse.

Susan... seven years of achievement and serenity... But, the role of 'Burton's wife' is far from easy... like riding sidecar on the wall of death... a woman can only take so much.

'Yet each man kills the thing he loves...' Oh Oscar! You put your finger on it boy..! You put your finger on it..!

We were making 'Wagner'... I... was making 'Wagner'... and during the seven months of filming... I began to look like Wagner, feel like Wagner... behave like Wagner... From the start of *my* Gotterdamerung, Susan lasted just four weeks.

It was then that one of the most shameful events of my life occurred. I took a drink... In fact... I... I suddenly hit it very hard...

Three *knights* later... *Sir* Larry Olivier, *Sir* Johnny Gielgud and *Sir* Ralph Richardson were flown out to join us for the filming...
I've always believed that once a king always a king, but... once a knight's enough...

I'd already had a row with some Italian cameraman - pretentious little toad. I told him 'Mickey Mouse' had better camera angles and he was giving me all this intellectual crap about the spiritual meaning of light and shade, which of course, I know everything about... I'm colour blind... And that night at dinner I reminded

Olivier that he'd once called me 'second rate'... Of course he denied it... He came on with 'But we all know you're the greatest actor in the world.' - A real put down...

'You call me second rate? You know the part you're playing in this film? You're playing a second-class minister, a second-class chief of police... It is a second-class role... I am Wagner. I am the star. The tables are turned!'

Yes, I told him... Why the hell did I do that?

He gets up and surveys the room

We're... making a film here.
Nineteen Eighty Four... The year I've been rehearsing for.
The part. It used to be fifty-eight vodkas and fifty eight-takes... but not now... Now I'm dry.
They've said I can use... the 'Richard Burton' voice... How very kind... I've been waiting to do a Burton.

Oh, and this?

He picks up a director's chair with his name, Richard Jenkins, on it.

How thoughtful... Now I can play second billing to myself...
What's in a name? 'Jen...kins'... Sounds like a bunch of gaoler's keys...
I'm rather fond of it... 'Richard Jenkins'...
George Orwell's name was Eric Blair... 'Eric Blair'... Some fairy from a troupe of prancing nancy-boys. With a name like 'Eric Blair'... he might have written 'Nineteen-Twenty One' but never *'Nineteen Eighty-Four'*.... Thank God Paul Scofield broke a leg... I'd told him he should often enough... This time he really did it... or rather a horse did it... So I play that evil swine from the 'Ministry of Truth'... O'Brien doesn't even get pleasure out of torture.

He sits

'*Do not imagine you will save yourself, Winston, however completely you surrender to us. No-one who has once gone astray is ever spared. And even if we chose to let you live out of the natural term of your life, still you would never escape us. What happens to you here is forever. Understand that in advance. We shall crush you down to the point from which there is no coming back. Things will happen to you from which you could never recover if you lived a thousand years... Never again will you be capable of love, or friendship, or joy of living, laughter, or curiosity, or courage, or integrity. You will be hollow... We shall squeeze you empty... And then we shall fill you with ourselves.*'

He addresses the director's chair

Could it be possible, I wonder, ever to do that? - Completely drain a man of his identity and create a totally new one? - Well, actors try... But how much of you survives?

Jenks! There's a lot of unemployment in these parts and I've got some bad news for you... I'm offering you a job.... No, not mining - mining is the pits, I know! There's not a lot of money in it... oh, only about seventy-five million. There, there lovely boy, I know its hard to bear... You'll have to sleep with the world's most beautiful women... Don't fret, there's worse to come... You'll play the Prince the way no Prince could dream of; your Kings will not be bettered by the best; you'll make the silence speak, the stillness move... You'll teach the English how to speak their lovely language... And all this, Jenks, shall be called an 'abdication', 'falling short' an 'unfulfilled ambition, unrealised potential!'... In fact, you'll 'never even come close'.

Ha, ha, hahaha! He says it's better than the haberdashery? So you'll take the job? Good boy, I knew I could rely on you... It's a great life... It's what you always wanted - What *we* always wanted for you...

He rises, slowly.

And now, as I am ready to come to terms with it all... finally to take possession of the essential core of my being, right now I am aware of the presence of a stranger...

He comes uninvited to my threshold, quite by chance, to deny me in that same spirit in which the gift was granted... without passion, without purpose, without drama. His sense of timing is sublime, artless...

'*... Gradually I was aware of someone in the doorway and turned my eyes that way and saw, carved out of the sunlight, a man who stood watching me... So still, there was not other such stillness anywhere on the earth... So... still... that the air seemed to leap at his side. He came towards me and the sun flooded its banks and flowed across the shadow. He asked me why I stood alone... His voice hovered on memory with open wings and drew itself up from a chime of silence, as though it had long-time lain in a vein of gold.*'

'*Tomorrow and tomorrow and tomorrow...*'

'*Our revels now are ended...*'

PLAYING BURTON was one of my very earliest efforts as a playright. It has had many hundreds of performances from Jerusalem to Budapest and New York with a few three to six-week runs in London and Edinburgh. In January 2001 it opened in Auckland and New York for two-year tours of New Zealand/Australia and the USA, with two different actors, Ray Henwood and Brian Mallon. It has never had a run in Wales.

The first draft was completed in 1986, but nothing really happened drama-wise until six years later. A thirty-five year old actor called Josh Richards turned up at a party for my daughter's birthday, pulled the script off the shelf and strolled up to me to ask if he could do it. He was so sure of himself. Bold as brass. Right build. Baritone voice. I just knew he was right for the part, because every time he spoke to me at the party, he slipped into Richard Burton mode with uncanny impersonation of that voice. Josh secured the services of director Hugh Thomas, a fellow Arsenal fan and brilliant theatre and TV director who subsequently became a good friend. Hugh simply loved the script and gave his time gratis to the long and difficult rehearsal sessions, even paying for the rehearsal space out of his own pocket. I soon realised that Josh's interpretation of the part went deep, way beyond mere impersonation.

The play received its first full professional performance at the London Festival of solo shows at the Etcetera theatre, Camden, produced by David Bidmead in a three-week run in Autumn 1992. Lindsay Anderson was one of the first to express his admiration for the piece. There followed a tour around various small venues in south and west Wales, including one at Port Talbot where most of the Burton clan turned out to give it their seal of approval.

Some time later, Josh met an old student friend, Guy Masterson (Burton's great nephew), who had given up science to run his own production company, Masterson Productions. Guy put the show on his repertoire after I had re-written some parts of it, and with Josh Richards starring, it toured small theatres all over England and Scotland, returning to Cardiff for one-night stands. Then it played at the Sybil Thorndike theatre before becoming a hit at the Edinburgh festival Assembly Rooms in 1994, largely due to Victor Spinetti drawing it to the attention of eminent critics like Jack Tinker of the Daily Mail. Victor was very taken with the play, the performance and the production and treated us all to champagne.

By now, Guy Masterson's shrewd direction and Josh's own learning curve had helped raise performances to even higher levels of sensitivity. As the play's reputation grew, Guy's skill as a producer was able to open doors that had previously remained shut to us. The show went on for a six-week run at the re-launched Riverside Studios, where Bill Burdett-Coutts praised it as 'the discovery of the Fesival'. Then it went to New York where it was showcased off- Broadway and contracted for two years. The deal fell through because of Green Card problems and American

Equity. 1997 found it again sold out at the Assembly Room for another three-week run. Steven Berkoff called backstage to pay us his respects and the reviews were the kind you dream of. A British Council funded tour then took it to Europe and the Far East before its star, Josh Richards, was signed up by the Royal Shakespeare Company. The play is currently being developed as a film screenplay.

The solo show is a real test for writer, actor and audience alike. Much is demanded of all concerned. Direction, lighting and sound acquire heightened, crucial dimensions. In 'Burton' I recommended three modes of performance woven like a plait. They are (a) The actor playing Burton-the-raconteur, talking about his life (b) Burton *acting* scenes from his life, and (c) Burton acting excerpts from his most celebrated theatrical and cinematic roles. All three modes have to be handled very differently and slipped in and out of, seamlessly. Some of the material is 'second-hand' but then Marlowe and Shakespeare never lose their value. The art lies in choosing just the right quotations to give tension and resonance to the experiences of Burton's life as it is being lived on stage, like chords to a melody line in music.

Writing a solo show is no mere autobiographical- chronology. Indeed these two dimensions can be death to the drama. What is important is not the order in which things actually happen in a rich and varied life but the underlying themes which provide clues to the meaning of the man. So, the predominant themes are Prince Hal, Lear and Faustus, which recur throughout like an ominous presence - Mephistopheles waiting for his due. Burton dies half-way through the play and reads his own obituaries. In life this kind of thing is, shall we say, rare; but what does it matter? If it works dramatically, do it. After all, everybody knows the great man died in 1984, so why not allow him to confront his critics posthumously?

The whole play is a search for identity - an ancient Welsh

preoccupation, from which even a minor playwright of Irish and Scots-Welsh ancestry cannot escape. Consider these elements in Burton's life. He gave up his surname, Jenkins. He gave up his father and became Philip Burton's adopted son. He gave up his first language for English. He even gave up his accent and developed a rich standard English delivered in classical tones. He left his homeland and settled in Switzerland. In choosing acting he lost himself in a thousand different roles. He developed a new persona. All his life he was 'Playing Burton', hence my title, which I infinitely prefer to the suggestion once made to me - 'Celtic Fury' - reminiscent of an unplaced horse in the three-thirty at Newmarket.

My thanks for the play's progress go to Josh Richards, Hugh Thomas, Guy Masterson, David Bidmead, Elaine James, Burton's generous family, Lewis Davies and the Arts Council of Wales.

Mark Jenkins.
Cardiff, November 2000.

Ed Thomas was born in Abercrâf. He has worked as a writer, director and producer. He is the founder director of both Y Cwmni and later Fiction Factory. His plays include *House of America* which won the Time Out 01 for London Award in 1989 and for which he also wrote the screenplay when it was filmed in 1997. Other plays include *East from the Gantry*, *The Myth of Michael Roderick*, *Flowers of the Dead Red Sea*, *Song from a Forgotten City* and *Gas Station Angel*. His work has been translated into several languages and been widely performed across Europe.

As a director and writer of stage, television and film he has won a number awards including the Welsh Writer of the Year, an Arts Foundation Fellowship Award, two BAFTA Wales Awards and Celtic Film Festival Awards for his films *Fallen Sons* and *A Silent Village*.

He lives in Cardiff.

Envy

Ed Thomas

Originally written as a monologue for television, *Envy* was adapted and produced by Fiction Factory where it toured all over Wales in 1993-5.

Ted John: **Russell Gomer**
Director: **Ed Thomas**

SCENE ONE

Ted John sits in his ramshackle caravan staring at an untouched boiled egg.

TED

It's just after six on a Sunday morning and this is Cwmgiedd, a one horse town in the heart of South Wales that's slap bang in the middle of a mystery. Some say it's the biggest mystery since the British flag and its flag pole were burnt down outside the Con Club after the '92 election and the culprit was never found. Others say it's the biggest since Glantawe Amateur Dramatic Society disbanded after their secretary and most experienced actress, Edna Davies, wife of Vicar David Davies and a woman of forty-five who should have known better, was found in an uncompromising position with Vic Small the garage's sixteen-year-old son Harry, during rehearsals for the Christmas panto, 'Mother Goose' five and a half years ago. Despite the fact that Vicar David Davies failed to find enough Christian Charity in his heart to forgive his wife for her sin and left her for a small parish in Abergavenny, leaving Edna to become a marriage guidance counsellor in Swansea and Harry Small becoming prematurely bald and taking up his post as a soldier in the Welsh Guards, most people say that this mystery is bigger and more serious by far. In short, Sid Lewis, local hero, local councillor, freemason, successful businessman and, if he plays his cards right, prospective MP, has disappeared into thin air, less than a week before he was due to appear as a 'Mastermind' contestant with Magnus Magnusson in a recording at the Brangwyn Hall in Swansea. Everybody round here is flabbergasted, the whole town is babbling. Ang, his wife, has made an appeal on telly, Glyn, his father, has spoken to the papers, and Magnus Magnusson himself has expressed his 'dismay and bewilderment' at what's happened and stresses that Sid, if found safe and well, will definitely be given a second opportunity at his earliest possible convenience. It hasn't stopped the recording mind you, they called in a retired vet from the Vale of Neath and the show kicks off at eight as planned. Everyone round here, including me, will be glued to their sets out of curiosity, and most will say poor old Sid, he should be there, he had the brains to win despite his lack of any formal further education. 'It's hell of a shame see,' said Jim Jones the papershop to me yesterday, but where is he? The last person to speak to him was Haydn Griffiths on the bridge over the Tawe around ten o'clock on Monday night. One of the town's great hill walkers is Haydn on account of the buzzing noise in his ears and the fresh air of the mountain stops him getting depressed and the wind deadens the sound he says. But no-one believes him. Everyone knows he walks the hills to avoid Moira his wife, who is still mourning the death of her idol, Roy Orbison. Moira's been known to sing 'Mystery Girl' into the early hours of the morning, the only real mystery is how she manages it after a bottle of vodka and two packets of slim panatellas. Anyway, all Haydn can say about his meeting with Sid that night was that Sid was in good spirits and was greatly looking forward to meeting Magnus Magnusson, a man he has long since respected and admired; so that any suspicion that Sid might have bottled out and lost his nerve have been quashed. Sid is no quitter; his best mate Micky Batts told the Drum and Monkey drinkers on Wednesday night, his record as Captain of the rugby team during a difficult period of re-building proves that, and everybody agrees. Then where the hell is he? Where is our Sid? Was he in debt? Is there another woman? Was he depressed? Has he fallen somewhere and lost his memory and even now is wandering lost and alone in some distant town? Has he heen kidnapped? Or worse, has he been murdered? Is there a maniac stalking this town who's committed an unspeakable crime? Is he a man the whole town knows but no-one suspects? The town is hanging on a knife edge. Sergeant Perkins and his three PC's are feeling the pressure. Their house-to-house enquiries have yielded a tidy haul of stolen property but no direct leads on Sid. Their only theory is that Sid left Haydn and took his usual walking the dog route down the canal bank, but as there are no signs of a scuffle and only scanty reports of the dog barking they can't be sure. So the mystery goes on. Everybody thinks it is odd. Very odd. Even... strange. Why would a man who had everything disappear before going on Mastermind? How can a man with a beautiful wife, two lovely kids, a dog, two cats, three Welsh ponies, two cars, a static caravan in a nice part of Pembroke, a speedboat, a swimming pool, a huge home with the biggest collection of sitting and standing gnomes this side of Swansea just DISAPPEAR INTO THIN AIR? Nobody knows, nobody has a clue, nobody, that is, except me.

SCENE TWO

Ted stands in a dark and run-down room containing four snooker tables.

TED

Ted John's the name, but most people call me Scon because it rhymes with John. It was Sid Lewis as it happens who first called me Scon in school and it stuck. Can't say I thank him for it, growing up in this Welsh Western town called Scon hasn't been without its difficulties. I'm pushing thirty, unmarried and I live on my own. I was born an only child to two ageing parents, my mother was forty and my father was fifty-five. I don't remember much about my father, he died when I was six, dropped dead in the Drum and Monkey in the middle of a darts match, two sets to one up he was too, in a five set final. They laid him out on the bar, called an ambulance, finished his pint for him and then finished the game. 'It's what he would have wanted us to do see', they told Evvie, my mother at the funeral, 'and at least he died when he was ahead'. We left our council house after that and moved in with Mam's brother... Uncle Ron. It wasn't the best of arrangements on account of Uncle Ron's obsession with disasters: travelled all over the country he has, following disasters. Mam told me not to judge him too harshly because of the trauma he suffered as a boy. Mam was still in her cot when it happened, Uncle Ron was ten and Ieu, his brother, was fourteen. My grandmother was making breakfast when Ieu picked up a loaded shotgun and shot her dead with both barrels. He never meant to do it, it was an accident, he'd been out hunting the day before and forgot to unload the gun. Growing up in Uncle Ron's house didn't do me much good either. I grew up a bit of a dreamer according to Mam with nothing much to say for myself. 'You've got to get out and mix a bit more Ted, or the world will leave you behind.' I took her advice and joined a few clubs, even thrown the odd dart in my time to see if any of my dad's skill had rubbed off on me, but I gave that up when I found I was ambidextrous and equally crap with each arm. I left school at sixteen with one O-level in woodwork but no love of wood and after a year on the dole I cut my losses and headed for the Smoke. Tooting was great aye. It had a common and the weather was better than it was here and who knows I might have got settled up there if it hadn't been for a phone-call from Uncle Ron. I was just settling down in my bedsit off the common when the phone rang. 'Hello,' I said. 'It's me,' said Ron. 'Alright Ron,' I said. 'No, your mother's had a heart attack,' said Ron. 'A what?' I said. 'You heard,' he said, 'now pack your bags and come home,' he said. 'But..' Then he slammed down the phone. Typical Ron that was. I caught the next train home and found Mam lying in bed but recovering. 'I'm feeling much better already now that you're home Ted,' she said. I smiled and supped my tea.

SCENE THREE

Ted stands in front of the remains of a pantomime set of Mother Goose.

TED

Two months later Mam was up and about eating less fat and no sugar in her tea when I heard some news that made my prospects look up. Glan Price, the caretaker of the Miner's Welfare Hall, decided to take early retirement and devote more time to his pigeons. 'It needs a young bloke with ideas to look atter that place,' he told me one day, 'but if you think you got what it takes Scon,' he said, 'apply to the committee'. I was the youngest applicant by twenty years and that, combined with my experience in the big city, swung it my way. It's a big responsibility running a place like this, the heart of the town: it had a library, a billiard hall, main hall for concerts, discos and pantos, the lesser hall down there for meetings and the spare room at the back when everything else was booked. For a couple of years it was like Piccadilly here, you couldn't keep people away, and then -

He clicks his fingers

- it changed. First they put the books from here in vans and called it the mobile library, then Amateur Dramatics split after the hullabaloo halfway through 'Mother Goose', then the Scouts set up headquarters in Oddfellow Street, and to cap it all, a bloke from the Midlands opened up a disco, restaurant and winebar place which finished the disco days here and sent the young, free and single flocking to his door. The only things that were left were the alternative theatre groups we had here from Cardiff, and even they went overboard not so long ago when Freddie Jones the butcher's son, Micky, brought a play he'd written down here, pulled in hell of a crowd too, with him being local and that. I don't know what all the fuss was about when I think of it now, it was the closest thing I'd come to seeing any woman nude since Mam fell awkward in the bath and I had to pull her out. By half time, half the crowd were on their way home, tut-tutting that they should have been warned about the nudes and bad language, and the other half, including Uncle Ron, came the second night as well, 'just to make sure the girl with the brown hair has got a tattoo where I think she's got a tattoo, see Scon.' She did alright, but tattoo or not, Freddie nearly went out of business when people started to boycott the shop in protest at the show, and he only saved his bacon when he started giving away free faggots with every Sunday joint over two pounds in money, and saying loudly and often enough, that the morals of the country were going down the pan. Just about saved his business that did, but it did nothing to save the hall. The only bloke who could do that was me. I knew its workings see, its possibilities. I knew I'd have to come up with my own project, a something special, and that's what I went home to do.

SCENE FOUR

Ted is back in the caravan watching TV.

TED

To be fair it was Mam in the end who hit the jackpot. She was sitting there one night tucking into some Turkish Delights when she pointed to the telly and said, 'You could do that see Ted'. 'Do what now Mam?' I said looking at the screen where a bloke with glasses was looking chuffed with himself. 'Do what that bloke Fred Housego's gone and done,' she said with a twinkle in her eye. 'He's an ordinary bloke, and he's just become Mastermind champion... see, there's Magnus Magnusson with him there, look.' I looked at the screen, looked at Magnus then at Fred: Mam was right, he was an ordinary looking bloke. 'You got to have brains,' I said. 'Brains run in this family,' said Mam, 'they just need pulling out a bit that's all. Imagine how proud you'd make me feel if I saw you up there winning a cut glass bowl from one of the top men on telly.' To be honest, my first reaction was to laugh and put it down to one of Mam's pipe-dreams. Besides I was a busy man, I had a welfare hall's interests to protect, and where was I going to get the time to do all the swotting and research and stuff? Then I thought about it again. And again and again. Fred Housego did it and he was a full-time taxi driver, he must have squeezed it in whenever he had a bit of free time, a bit of reading, a bit of burning the midnight oil. The more I thought about it, the only difference between me and Fred was our accent! I decided to throw caution to the wind and give it a go! A flame was lit inside me that night. A flame that I've kept alight for seven years. Seven years that started when I walked into the house with the Encyclopedia Britannica under one arm, Daily Mirror and One Thousand Sporting Fact and Figures under the other, a smile on my face, Mam in her oils and Uncle Ron looking at me as if I was a disaster that was just about to happen. 'You should never have encouraged him Evvie,' he said to Mam, 'I've seen more brains in a tin of Chum.' Mam laughed and just said, 'Let him have a go'. Fair play to Mam. She defended me to the hilt, gave me all the support any budding Mastermind contestant could ever ask for, tested me on the millions of facts, figures, dates, names, places, books, people, the lot, all the information I needed to become a champion. It was her that persuaded me to take a dozen books on Greek Mythology away with us to Blackpool... for the last summer holiday she ever had on this earth... Losing her on an early summer day three years ago nearly made me throw in the towel.

PAUSE

But the thought of being alone in the house with Uncle Ron's stories for the next twenty years gave me the spur to carry on. It was half-way through a tale of a gas explosion in Briton Ferry that I told him I was moving into the caravan for a bit of peace and quiet, to concentrate on my challenge. He wasn't happy about it, especially when I told him I wasn't going to encourage visitors, but I had no choice. For a year I made good progress, then Sid Lewis crossed my path when he decided to build his new house in the field in front of me. He complained to the council and everything, saying my caravan was an eyesore and I'd have been evicted too if it hadn't been for Harry Gwyn whose field I parked on. Harry stuck by me out of loyalty to my father, after all it was him who finished dad's pint for him on the day he died in the Drum and Monkey. He's been great to me has Harry, and if he hadn't been in his eighties, I'd have happily called him a mate of mine, but he's still the only bloke I've ever told I was applying for Mastermind. 'Mastermind?' said Harry, 'you're talking big time boy, big time. Have you got a specialist subject then?' 'Yes,' I said, 'Cwmgiedd Miners Welfare Hall, the complete and comprehensive history from 1918 to the present day...' Harry wasn't too convinced in the beginning, 'There's not enough history there mun to keep Magnus happy!' 'It's not the specialist subject that's the real test Harry, it's the general knowledge that sorts the men from the boys and I got more of that in my head than any bugger!' 'You know best Ted I suppose, I just hope you know what you're doing.' He wished me all the best, and what's more knows how to keep a secret ... but even Harry never knew that I asked Magnus to put on a show in the Welfare Hall.

SCENE FIVE

Ted walks on a rubbish tip to the sound of scavenging gulls and a distant bulldozer. He reads from a letter.

TED

Dear Mr Magnusson,

The big, posh halls in universities that you do your shows in are lovely, but they put a lot of ordinary people like me off. We don't feel as if we belong there see, and it gives the professional people, like the Chemists and the Teachers, a big advantage, because they're used to places like that and we're not. Writing as I am as the caretaker of the Miners Welfare Hall, I'd like to say that it would be a perfect place for Mastermind to go on. There's plenty of room on the floor if you don't want to do it on the stage, and you can put the audience round the sides as usual. We've also got lights here and cheese and wine can be made available for the chat afterwards, or if necessary, we can always ask Mr Derek Davies - who has his own equipment - to provide a varied and exciting disco.

Yours faithfully, Ted John (Caretaker).

Suggesting the Welfare Hall was a last minute thing. I didn't think Magnus would go for it, but he didn't know the possibilities of the Welfare like me, and besides, I had nothing to lose, in fact, everything to gain. I'd be on home territory, and if I won, I'd be a hero overnight, the boy from nowhere just like Tom Jones. I started thinking about the benefits victory would bring; Magnus would invite me over to his house where he'd tell me tales of his native Iceland long into the night. I'd have a model for a girlfriend who'd wait for me in posh hotel rooms with bottles of champagne and the answer which won me the Mastermind final on her full red lips: 'The first chairman of the Welfare Hall was Wilfred Parsons, died in 1931 of pneumoconiosis' she'd say with a smile, then I'd dive under the silk sheets with her and eat her.

Ted crumples up the letter and throws it.

TED

But it never happened. They said no to my application and no to doing it in the Welfare. I went through all the emotions that day that any man can, apart from happiness. What hurt me most is that Magnus never even read the letter. One of the Mastermind team did I suppose. After all the effort I'd put in, it hurt, it hurt a lot.

Ted reads

Dear Mr John,

Thank you for your letter and application form, but unfortunately due to the overwhelming response and the extremely high quality of applications we received, we are unable to find room for you in our regional short-list this year. We would like to take this opportunity to thank you for your interest and your kind suggestion that we record an episode in a Welfare Hall, but our arrangements this year have already been completed.

Yours sincerely, Angelica Davidson.

Ted throws away the letter.

Angelica Davidson! What sort of a name is that I said to Sergeant Perkins that night when he locked me in the cell for being drunk and disorderly, and fair play to him asked me if I was having woman trouble. I nearly told him the whole story, but looking back on it now it's a bloody good job I didn't. My Mastermind secret died with Harry Gwyn, two days before last Christmas he passed away the way he lived most of his life, causing no fuss or bother to anyone.

SCENE SIX

Ted walks onto the stage in the Welfare Hall amongst the tattered curtain and old pantomime bric-a-brac.

TED

Christmas came and Christmas went. I went to Freddie's and bought myself a turkey. Uncle Ron came over on Boxing Night for old times' sake and drank all my whisky, and I let him ramble on till he fell asleep halfway through a lifeboat disaster in Devon. The only other person who's called since has been Sergeant Perkins, the day before yesterday, wanting to know when was the last time I'd seen Sid and did I know anything of his disappearance. I wasn't surprised to see him call mind you, I was the obvious suspect on account of me being an outsider, a bit of a loner, but he went away after a cup of tea and a biscuit, with no more information than he came in with. I've read enough crime stories full of facts and figures in the last seven years, see, to know full well how to handle a desperate policeman in search of a suspect: deny all knowledge, be as helpful as possible and tell him how everybody in town thinks he's doing a good job. Anyway, by February I was starting to feel better. Winter was nearly over and spring was coming. I was even re-applying with a new specialist subject and a letter with a notice on the front saying 'not to be opened by Angelica Davidson' when I saw a headline in the paper in Jim Lewis's papershop that made me stop dead in my tracks. 'LOCAL VALLEY BUSINESSMAN TO APPEAR ON MASTERMIND' said the headline and there next to it was a picture of Sid, Ang and the kids, smiling into the camera. 'It's great innit,' said Jim, 'it couldn't happen to a nicer bloke.' Nicer bloke! My head nearly exploded. 'If he's the best bloke to represent this town on Mastermind, Jim,' I said, starting to stammer, 'then... S...S... Stalin and Hitler weren't the tyrants they were but... Church Wardens!' 'In Germany and Russia!' and I stormed out of the shop with my words ringing in the air. He's never been the same to me since either but how was a man like me supposed to cope with such an obvious injustice? I was easily better than Sid Lewis. I'd just have to go out and prove it to the rest of the town, that's all.

PAUSE

But how?

PAUSE

After a long session of playing snooker with myself, the left arm versus the right, the solution came to me, like that. I'd organise my own special Mastermind, here, in the Welfare Hall!

SCENE SEVEN

Ted peers from behind a curtain.

TED

This is where it all happened, the Lesser hall, a meeting place, it's not too big, not too small, intimate I'd call it. There are the people who came.

Ted pulls away the curtain to reveal a sea of faces painted on the back of an old pantomime set. They are badly painted caricatures, but Ted seems very happy with them, even proud.

Everybody was here, Haydn 'Buzz in the Ear' Griffiths, Moira his wife, Jim Lewis, the papershop down here, Clive from the bank, John Hickey and his wife, Edna, Beti Webb, a few old friends from school, the whole town. It turned into a real event. Mam was here as well, come back from the dead sitting next to Harry Gwyn, I had to make sure I'd got Turkish Delights in to keep her happy.

PAUSE

I painted them myself on the back of the Mother Goose set, worked a treat it has, bought the paints top-price from Evans the Ironmongers, everything's top-price in that shop, but it's been worth it, took me a month and a half, a hundred and thirty-one faces all together.

Ted reveals the Mastermind chair.

The chair cost me an arm and a leg. I had it specially delivered. I'm still paying for it in monthly instalments. I bought it in Swansea in a furniture shop in the arcade. The assistant there said he suffered bouts of migraine and sitting in a soft expensive leather chair like this helped him relax, soothe the pain. He said it was a must for anyone living in the Mumbles with a nice view of the sea; I told him I lived in a caravan in the valleys, he said the thought of that made his migraine worse, and got someone else to serve me. He was a snob, but I still bought the chair. I mean, you can't have a Mastermind without a black leather chair can you?

Ted reveals a dummy with a suit on behind a tatty desk.

And this is Magnus. It took me a day and a half and the best part of a week's newspapers to make him and he still didn't turn out as well as I expected. It was my fault for not buying him a proper suit I suppose, but time was short and money was tight, so in the end I had to make do with an old one of Uncle Ron's. With Magnus finished and sat in his chair waiting for action, my preparation was complete. I had a crowd, a chair, a question master and one contestant - me. We were all ready for the showdown. This was going to be a Mastermind with a difference, a two-horse race. The missing horse was Sid Lewis. I didn't want anyone else involved. Just me and Sid, alone.

SCENE EIGHT

Down at the canal bank, Ted throws a stone into the river.

TED

Getting Sid on his own was harder than I thought, but living so close to his house meant that I could keep a close watch on his comings and goings. Sid likes to take Butch, the dog, for a walk around ten o'clock. He'd walk over the Tawe bridge, down the canal bank, back over the Teddy Bear bridge and home. This is where I'd make my approach. My first problem was Butch, he's a big dog and I didn't fancy tangling with him. Then I noticed that Sid as a rule let him off the lead as soon as they reached the canal bank and Butch liked to run ahead, sometimes a hundred yards or more, and what was more important, he did it every time. I decided I'd provide him with a bit of supper, a couple of mice I'd caught in the Welfare Hall mixed in with a few dog biscuits. I'd wait for Butch to clear, then I'd get to Sid. It worked like magic. I parked the van by Beti Webb's house which stands in front of a little wood leading to the canal bank. I went down the canal bank at about nine with a stocking to cover my head, and I took some chloroform we kept in the Welfare Hall to clean the floors with and a huge wad of cotton wool. I got that idea from a film to be honest, some spy story with Michael Caine in it. I waited for an hour and a half before I saw any sign of him. I watched him talk to Haydn on the bridge and then I saw Haydn move away home. Then Sid started walking towards the canal bank. I started to feel nervous. My hands started to shake, my mouth felt dry, I told myself to relax. He was coming closer, Butch ran on ahead as I'd hoped. Sid stopped to light a fag. For a moment I thought I couldn't go through with it, but then I imagined what it would be like sitting there watching Sid answer Magnus's questions in the Brangwyn Hall in a fancy suit and concentrated expression, and my blood boiled. As Sid came within six feet of me, I checked to see where Butch was, he was barking and out of sight. 'The dog has found the mouse,' I said to myself, time to make my move. I crept up behind him, while his fag was still in his hand, I brought my arm up around his neck and brought the other arm with the chloroform up over his face. I squeezed for what like seemed forever. I was sure Michael Caine hadn't taken this long to pass out, but maybe the temperature had something to do with it. He passed out in the snow in Russia. Sid eventually slumped into my arms on a mild evening of late May in South Wales. His fag fell to the floor and burnt in the grass, I picked it up and threw it in the river, a detail any KGB man would have been proud of. Butch was still barking somewhere along the canal but Sid was in my hands and helpless. Five minutes later he was in the back of the van and we were heading towards the Welfare.

SCENE NINE

Ted pushes on a wheelchair.

TED

I brought him in through the back door, tied him in this wheelchair and gagged him. Then I pushed him through to the theatre of operations into the lesser hall, where the black chair, Magnus and the painted faces of the crowd were waiting. I wheeled him into position over there and sat down to wait. I reckoned the chloroform would wear off in about a quarter of an hour and Sid would be failing to answer the questions I set him. I was going to sit behind Magnus and ask him questions based on the Welfare Hall as a specialist subject before hitting him with the general knowledge ones. I was looking forward to watching him sweat, struggling to answer, embarrassing himself in front of the crowd, making himself a laughing stock, a fool, confessing to everyone in the town that despite all the advantages he'd had in life, I, Ted John, better known as Scon, was a better contender than he was. Then I was going to keep him here till the recording with the retired vet from the Vale of Neath had been done, wait for the fun to die down, sell the caravan and use the money to get myself set up in the Smoke. I'd never really given myself an even break up there and I hadn't seen it since the day Mam had her heart attack. Once settled safely up there, I was going to phone up Sergeant Perkins, put on a phoney voice and tell him where Sid was hidden. By the time Sid would have told the whole town what I'd done, I'd be safe in the warrens of the metropolis, with a new name, a new identity and a new life. I'd grow myself a beard and who knows, get some specs with clear lenses, the possibilities for me were endless.

PAUSE

Except, that I would never be able to go on Mastermind, and I would never have been able to make Mam happy. The best I would be able to do is go on 'Brain of Britain' with Robert 'Ask the Family and Call my Bluff' Robinson. But even that would be risky. What if I'd won and been crowned with the Brain of Britain, I'd be a celebrity even with a false name. They'd ask me to go on talk shows, 'Aspel', 'Parkinson', even 'Clive Anderson'. I should have thought of it earlier, but I was too obsessed with making sure Sid never got on Mastermind: it was the only hole in an otherwise watertight plan. Meeting Magnus and winning Mastermind was Mam's dream that night seven years ago, not Robert Robinson and the Brain of Britain; winning the cut glass bowl from the top man on the telly and not the top man on the radio. My mind was made up. If I was to realise Mam's dream and win the cut glass bowl to put Turkish Delights in it in memory of her, my plan would have to change completely. I'd have to make sure that Sid Lewis never spoke again.

PAUSE

I had to make a snap decision. Sid was already starting to come round, grunting at first, then moving his head. I had no time to waste. He'd be awake I reckoned in less than a minute. I put my hands round his neck and applied equal pressure to both sides 'til both of us were blue in the face. He must have liked living a lot, he took longer than I thought to die. He opened his eyes and I watched the cocktail parties, the orgies, Magnus, the questions and the garden gnomes all flit by in the glassy lights of his eyes. He reminded me of the way the butterfly I murdered when I was nine must have felt before I pulled off his wings and watched him fall like a stone into an orange tulip in Uncle Ron's garden.

PAUSE

And then all of a sudden the pictures stopped. Everything was quiet. Sid was still looking up at me but his eyes were lifeless.

PAUSE

The show was over. I shut them quickly and let go of his neck, he fell to the floor in a heap.

Ted topples over the wheelchair.

SCENE TEN

Ted sits in his caravan staring at a boiled egg.

TED

I gave Sid a temporary grave in the cellar of the welfare.

PAUSE

He'll be safe enough until October. The dust will have settled by then, and the mystery of Sid Lewis will be forgotten in the rush towards Christmas. When the time is right I'll drive my van over there, dig him up and take him over to the field behind his house where I'll bury him...forever. It would be nice if I gave him a gravestone, one of his gnomes maybe, the one with the fishing rod: but I don't suppose I will. There'd always be someone who'd want to know what a gnome was doing in the corner of a field and report it to Sergeant Perkins.

PAUSE

I'm expecting him to call soon, drink a cup of tea, ask a few questions...the usual. When he does, I'll tell him that I'm thinking of applying for Mastermind's next series in honour of Sid: who knows I might even win and make Mam's dream come true, make myself a hero in the town. In the meantime I'll keep things to myself, and keep eating my boiled eggs, because as Mam always said, 'nothing settles a nervous stomach like a boiled egg.'

Looks at the egg. He doesn't move.

Ian Rowlands was born in Porth in the Rhondda. He trained as an actor before turning to writing. He was the founder director of Theatr Y Byd and since 1992 has written eight full length plays including *Blue Heron in the Womb*, *Glissando on an Empty Harp* and *Love In Plastic*.

His credits for radio and television include *A Light in the Valley* which won a Royal Television Society Award. He is currently Artistic Co-ordinator of Bara Caws - a national community touring Welsh language theatre company.

He lives in Cardiff.

Marriage of Convenience

Ian Rowlands

Man	Gareth Potter
Director	Ian Rowlands
Designer/	
Production Manager	David Roxburgh
Stage Manager	Daryl James

The play first opened on a snowy evening at Coleg Meirion Dwyfor, Dolgellau on the 19th November 1996. It was originally booked in ten community venues throughout Wales. Four years later it is approaching its hundredth performance. In 1997 it won a Herald Angel award at the Edinburgh Festival, the Dublin Dry Gin Award for best play at the Dublin Festival and Gareth Potter was nominated as best actor in the Stage Awards for his performance. It has attracted widespread media attention and has been the subject of two television documentaries.

Night. Dawn reveals a rock which hangs above the valley as if suspended from the clouds. Dogs bark. A man stands.

VOICEOVER

There were June days spent sitting on my Sunday sanctuary.

Half way to heaven, and the top twenty harmonising with the screams of babies that floated up from the valley floor; screams that mingled with the irony of mocking dogs and the war cries of crows tapping phone lines with their feet.

There were nights spent on the Whiterock reading omens in the disappearing clouds. Sardis Road, as dead as The Beatles beneath me, and the neon G of the Graig corkscrewing out of the cwm towards Beddau, The Lamb and Flag and beyond.

Then there were Saturday afternoons on the cusp between the Rhondda and the Ogmore Valleys. In the back of a Hillman Minx, sandwiched between two aunts carving cornets with dry lips, I sucked a chocolate Oyster, bigger than the the town of Treorchy beneath me.

Moments on mountains. A Valley's childhood, volumes one to eighteen; the chronicle of any poor dab who wants to touch a sky that stretches from horizon to horizon not just from Glynfach to Llwyncelyn. Faced with mountains, we have to climb them. What else can we do bar scramble out of the dark and into the light; it's instinctive for a kid born in the shade to strive for the sun.

MAN

When I woke up that morning, it was half past nine. I banged on a tape and Bauhaus were proclaiming, 'The sky's gone out'. As far as I knew perhaps it had. Perhaps the Valley had been struck by a meteor overnight and the dust of all dead fathers had risen to blanket the sun. My mother barged in on my erection: 'If you were a woman you'd be a slut,' she said with more than a hint of resentment on her tongue. I stuck in her eyes like a truck full of grit and I felt that at that moment, she would've liked to have scythed my face... if only I wasn't her son; a ghost's child who saw a million faces in the clouds and called each one of them father.

My dad was dead. Drunk one night in the port of Brake unter Weser, he slipped between the gang plank and the quay. Floundering for a few moments in the water between the dock and the ship, he struggled for a grip, anything that would offer him safety, but there was nothing. I know, because I floated in the dock beside him. I saw the fear on his face as the ship edged towards the key, squeezing his bones and flesh, 'til the pressure popped his eyes like two clogged ketchup bottles giving up the ghost and drowning a meal.

There again perhaps he was eaten by a hammer headed shark in Lake Superior within spitting distance of Duluth, knifed in a bar over a side of beef in Buenos Aires or boiled to death in a mud pool in Rotorua. Wherever he died, I was there; sitting, standing, floating next to him as he grinned the grin of a fox caught in the headlights of a Winter's evening.

To my mother, the where and the how were irrelevant. That's all that mattered to her was that he wasn't around, any more and she hadn't forgiven him for going. Without so much as a bye or a leave he buggered off leaving only his fossils in my face; my nose, my eyes, my mouth were a daily reminder of her loss, the growing paradox of her pain. There was resentment in her voice that morning when she pulled back the curtains to reveal the day of the Royal Wedding, July the twenty-ninth, nineteen eighty-one.

'I hope you've changed your mind about today, or there'll be hell of a stink,' she said. 'You know what he's like and I don't want any shenanegans, Alex. He'll just play up and I couldn't cope with it, not today of all days.'

By 'he', she meant 'Him', my stepfather. He had a name all right, but I was buggered if I was going to call him by anything which made him human.

'He' slunk into our life when I was ten, two years after my father's death. 'He' jammed his foot in the door of our family like a Jehovah's Witness who'd spotted a crack and was about to squirm in.

One morning, I ran into my mother's bedroom expecting an early morning kiss, an understandable expectation for the only son of a dead father, but that morning, her kisses were for other lips.

'This is Andrew,' she said, and hey presto, he was there; reclining in my father's shadow as if he owned the bed; door mat for a chest, an Osmond smile and eyes that sparkled like slate in the rain.
He picked a hair from his lip and tried to lasso me with a grin. I clocked hypocrisy for the first time in my life. I have seen it many times since, too many. I remember when I was about fourteen, my mother saw the stains on my morning sheets and packed me off to a Christian for a chat. 'To make love is a sacred act between man and wife,' The Christian said, Devils for teeth, 'A man's seed is the seed of God, each seed is sacred.' His wife sat in the corner as bored as a pod in a drought.

'This is Andrew,' my mother said, crowning him with squeeze of her hand, and that was that. I guess you can't cuddle a slow cooling memory for ever. I suppose my mother had human needs, but I didn't want to recognise the woman in her. She was a Goddess and I was a pubeless Oedipus. How dare 'He' come between the three of us; my father's ghost, my mother and me. I hated him instantly. It might have been the way he stroked my mother's hair as if he was stroking a horse across a fence, or it might have been the way he stuck daggers around their love with his stare; a big screaming 'Verboten' of a stare. Fuck off, don't come near.

'Come and give your mam a big hug,' she said, but there was an unfamiliar smell of stale flannel and toilets in the air, I shook my head and left. There was no place for me in their bed. He'd planted mines around it and there was a machine gun nest between the sheets. 'Oh God! I know we shouldn't have. Not so soon,' I heard my mother say as I legged it across the landing. 'Don't worry love, he'll come round to the idea,' 'He' said.

A year or so after discovering the cuckoo in the nest, I still hadn't come round to the idea. They married anyway, and almost at once, his duck arse smile loosened in proportion to the iron grip he began to exert upon us. We became prisoners of his toddler tyranny; his tantrums, more tantrummy than mine. For God's sake, he was the grown man, I was the kid of eleven! His emotions ruled all days. He became a little Napoleon exiled in our Elba, he ruled us like his empire. I had a perfect hate for him, and I felt that deep down, my mother shared at least a part of my loathing, if only when plates shattered against walls and words were spoken.

'I hope to God you've changed your mind about today?' my mother sighed, 'Breakfast is ready, don't be long about it.' She left me lying on my bed, staring through the window at the mountain; one third blue, two thirds green.

The mountain puckered to kiss the sky with promiscuous lips. It was the first thing I saw each morning and the last thing I couldn't see at night as I closed the curtains on another day. Always there, it challenged me to follow sheep trails to the top and glimpse an horizon that stretched from Porthcawl to Brecon.

As a short trousered kid, I was tied to the foothills by my mother's eyes. But in time, and with my mother's say so, I struck out for base camp on the flat. There, where the crows blind lambs, our kites played chicken with power lines and Cardiff City beat Brazil a thousand times before I was allowed to climb on, up onto the tump.

Overnight, and with cricket bats in case the 'Banog kids came, I charred bangers, listening to the tales of Valley Vasco da Gamas who'd been to the top, bottom front and bottom back. They'd seen sights I could only dream of seeing until it was my time to climb on. And when it was, I picked my way through ferns and black wimberries and struck out for the top.

It's the last few steps before reaching the peak that make a climb worth the craic; the expectation, like the moment before unwrapping a present from Auntie Sheila on Christmas morning. Unwrapped, it's invariably a disappointment; a pair of socks, a bottle of Brut deodorant. But wrapped, its full of promise; a curate's egg before it's cracked.

When you reach the peak, you want to climb into the sun, but there is no higher to climb without sprouting wings and flying. So you climb back down and search for a higher mountain. I went down to the kitchen.

In the kitchen 'He' sat munching a massacre. 'Got to line the stomach kid,' he said. Bits of bacon flew from his mouth and greeted me French fashion upon each cheek. I wiped the flesh away and poured myself a bowl of Klondike Pete's.

'Looking forward to the street party then?' he asked shovelling the black pudding in. I ignored him and concentrated on the Golden Nuggets yellowing my milk.
'Fancy some toast, Alex?' my mother said changing the subject.
'I'll have some, love,' he said. 'It's going to be a day and an half today, I want a breakfast and an half to set me up for it. What

about you kid? You want to keep your strength up for the party mun.'

'I'm not hungry,' I said. 'But, it's going to be a long day, don't be stupid,' he spat through chewed meat. I wanted to scream his flesh from his face, 'I am not fucking stupid!' I had been stupid to him since the day dot.

When I wanted to watch Jackanory, I was stupid; when I sucked peas for ten minutes because I couldn't swallow them, I was stupid; when I lost my football boots on the bus, I was stupid; even when I was dying, or thought I was dying from a rare form of something or other, I was stupid. I had nothing between my ears, as thick as shit, a daft bugger, twp as tuppence, a no-hoper, just plain bloody stupid.

I wanted my mother to plant my flag in his skull, like a human Iwo Jima, Wham! But she rarely did. Though in the rare moments we shared together, she used to hold me tight and reassure me that I was not as dense as the darkness in his skull. I was a bright star and I shone only for her.

Once, he eavesdropped upon our intimacy. My mother was squeezing me tight as a wrung sock when he popped out from no-where, my mother jumped clean out of her skin. 'You're bloody stupid,' he said, 'The boy's fourteen, stop mothering him. You don't want a bloody poof for a son do you? Go out and play with the boys mun, stop being so bloody stupid.'

'You're the stupid one, Andrew,' my mother said. 'I'm not stupid,' 'You are stupid,' 'I'm not bloody stupid, you're the bloody stupid one,' he said on the verge of a tantrum.

'All right I'm bloody stupid. If you can't beat the stupid, join them.'

Brain the speed of a Spectrum, realisation slowly dawned across his face. 'Well thanks a bunch, love.' He went off in a huff. My mother smiled and we hugged. 'Don't take a blind bit of notice of him, Alex,' she said. 'Sometimes I wonder who's the adult, you or him?' 'I bloody heard that!' came from the kitchen. 'Then serves you right for listening,' my mother replied. 'Bloody stupid...' we heard him muttering. I had been stupid to him from the beginning.

'Get some toast down your neck, mun.' 'I am not hungry,' I said. 'Suit yourself then.'

He ploughed a furrow through a field of scrambled eggs.

On the formica kitchen units my mother was preparing the loaves and fishes; salmon sandwiches to feed the multitudes that would descend upon the trestle tables like old age piranhas upon a jumble sale.

Her Pyrex plates were piled high as tips with neat little triangles of white bread and pink paste. 'There'll be plenty to eat at the party,' she said, 'Perhaps Alex'll be hungry then.' 'For God's sake love, you're too bloody soft by half to that kid,' 'He' grunted and munched on. My mother shook her head as if to say 'He's not worth the bother.' If he wasn't worth the bother why did she bother putting up with him?

The kitchen echoed to the sound of pig eating pig; a symphony of cannibalism. When you abhor someone, every slurp or half dribble is annoying. He licked a blob of suet from his chin. I pushed my Klondike Pete's to the side and said, 'I'm not going to the street party'; silence of a frozen hell. 'You what!' he shouted, crashing both knife and fork into his plate. 'And where the hell are you going then?' 'To a picnic', I said. 'So, he's going to a picnic, is he? There's nice for him. Street party's not good enough for you is it kid?'

'Don't start Andrew.' 'Don't bloody start! He's the one that bloody started it.' I stood up. 'Sit down, I'm talking to you, kid.' My mother sighed an 'Oh God' into her sandwich paste. 'What bloody picnic?' he said.

The picnic was on top of a mountain. I told him that I was going with Jez and his family. The word 'family' slipped surreptitiously through my lips like a fart in the bath.

'So he's going with his family, is he? We're not good enough for you, is that it?' 'That's not the point,' I protested. He picked up his fork and stabbed his point home with it: 'So what is the point then kid?'

I choked on a half chewed apology, 'It's a Welsh picnic.' The munching stopped. He looked at me and grunted through grease, 'Bloody thought so! If I had my way you would never have gone to that bloody Welsh school. Bunch of fanatics, that's all they are. Just be glad I'm not your father kid.' My mother closed her eyes and melted.

'Welsh is a waste of bloody time. Your dad should've had his head seen to, mun'. 'He' loved roasting my father on the spit of his criticism; killing him again and again in front of the woman who had loved him. Out of embarrassment, a glass shattered upon the floor. 'Now look what you've made your mother do. You're bloody useless, help her clear it up, mun.'

'I've said it all along, and I'll say it again, that Welsh school is just an Academy of Fascists.' He relished the word 'fascist' as only a bigot can. 'I'd rather hack my leg off than learn Welsh mun. No bugger speaks Welsh in the Valleys, face it.' I wanted to say 'Don't be so stupid', but I didn't have a leg to stand on, I shed my language each night like a linguistic snake, most of my friends did.

When I was a kid, Welsh was just a shift language; nine to four Monday to Friday with overtime on Thursdays for club; it was a Cinderella language, it didn't live beyond the school gates.

If you spoke Welsh in Blaenllechau or Blaencwm, you might as well've been speaking Latin. You could hear people talking about you behind your back: 'What language are they speaking then? Perhaps they're German on a school trip.'

Then they'd twig, 'No, they're the crachach from the Welsh school, aren't they. Who the hell do they think they are, eh? This is Wales, why can't they speak the majority language like the rest of us? Bloody annoying.' We were given a language all right, but not the social context to place it within.

It was different for some; friends like Jez. Because in Welsh language schools there are two sorts of kids; those that come from Welsh speaking homes and those that don't. Jez did, I didn't; his Welsh was sterling, mine was guilt. He had an automatic in on the whole Welsh thing.

Our friendship was built on harmonised versions of Bohemian Rhapsody sung outside the continually broken school swimming pool. One free lesson offered us the chance of a Night at the Opera, a double, A Day at the Races and overnight at his parents we could strain our larynxes to the whole Queen repertoire.

I loved staying with his family; the smell of toast and the sound of Radio Cymru on the Bakelite radio every morning. I didn't even know there was a Welsh radio station before staying with them.

I remember one weekend, they took me to their family home in Dyfed; Edward H Dafis on the mono player and the dust of bourgeoisie neglect hanging on shafts of lazy sunlight. Conversations with farmers, not understanding the dialect; daubing signs green, not grasping the argument, just beginning to realise that Welsh wasn't a dead vocabulary to be wiped off the blackboard with contempt.

Because being sent to Welsh school can be like the gift of a computer without the instruction book, the cross without the guilt; you've got something, but you don't know what the hell it is, or what the hell to do with it.

Jez and his family were my missing manual; through them I began to put the language into context, make sense of the whole Welsh thing. One weekend in Dyfed can make sense of a whole education.

'Stop bloody day dreaming and help your bloody mother,' he barked, a baked bean shot from the cannon of his lips. My mother shooed me as I walked towards her, 'Go to your friend's and have a nice time at the picnic, I'll deal with this,' - by 'this' she meant 'him'. I grabbed my motorbike helmet and left the kitchen.

Before they built a bypass, there was a bend on the Ponty side of Trehafod where the road used to widen. On my motorbike, I'd tail cars through Trehafod village, past the dead pit where my uncle caught cancer, down the hill where houses bend like old women's backs, and across the green iron bridge. A strict thirty, past the two-inch gap that separated two houses and two boroughs, and on past the pub with pigeons in its rafters and the chip shop next to it. At the bottom end of the village, the road narrowed into an S bend around a graveyard then widened as it left the dead behind.

Slipping out of the S, I'd ram the gears into third and torture the engine. Then I'd pull back the throttle and I'd be flying; past cars, past caring. Flying to Ponty and beyond. Like leaping off a mountain.

VOICEOVER

Once, I dreamt I was on top floor of an unfinished sky-scraper, a trespasser in the empire of the wind. Securing each hand hold, I edged towards the unglazed windows and willed myself to peer over the edge. Slowly, my field of vision dropped from the sky to the horizon and approached me across a cityscape, like a cloud's shadow passing over the land.

When it reached the vertical, I wanted to fly down and embrace the focus; a dangerous feeling, and I sensed that I was about to succumb, so I tilted up my gaze and rested it upon the safety of the horizon.

Suddenly, the world flipped ninety degrees and in my line of descent lay the sun. There was no further need for this Icarus to worry about wax, I could just give myself over to the infinite possibilities and step into the horizon.

MAN

My wings were clipped that morning as I turned the corner by the graveyard. The 332 was coming in the opposite direction. So I let the throttle go and cruised behind a car.

As soon as I arrived at Jez's, I left again. Five of us crammed into a Mini and made tracks North to the Valleys of Gwent. We were on our way to see an old FWA member who'd served time for a nation, half of which didn't consider him a compatriot and the other half didn't give a damn. He'd even campaigned for a language he couldn't even speak.

Half an hour later, in a town with no name, we pulled up in a terrace tacked to the side of a mountain like an afterthought. Tricolour bunting threaded it, binding two pavements together for the occasion. The prematurely fading faces of Charles and Diana hung in double glazed windows and chairs sat patiently under a dead dog sun waiting for fat arses to sit down on them.

We piled out of the car. Four followed, the one who knew the right bell to ring. He rang, and we hung loose, like bailiffs eager for a fight. The door opened, and a woman holding a kid stood defiant. 'What do you want?' she said.
'Is your husband...' We didn't get the chance to say any more, she wiped the floor with us, 'Don't you talk to me about my husband, you've probably got more of an idea where he is than I have. I haven't seen him for two days and I've got three hungry mouths to feed. Money don't grow on trees you know. What the hell do

you want with him anyway?'

'We were wondering whether he was going to the picnic?' 'What picnic?' she asked, 'The Republican picnic' someone blurted out.

'I bloody knew it!' 'she screamed. 'I knew it would be some bloody Welsh thing or other, today of all sodding days, bloody par for the course. I'm sick to death of all your Welsh shit. Why can't you just get your claws out of my husband and leave him be mun? He's done enough for your sodding cause already. Free bloody Wales, that's a bloody joke. I've paid my whole bloody marriage for it, I can't afford to pay any more.'

I stood close enough to smell her fear run down her hair, drip onto the floor and emulsify in a slick around her plastic feet. Her child started to cry at her hip. From across the street a voice called. 'Joyce love, are you all right?'

'Right as rain, Cliff. Now just bugger off and give me my husband back. I want him back here, yesterday, you listening? You tell him that when you see him. If he's not back here pronto, he's out on his arse this time. That's my final warning. Do you hear me?'

She looked directly into my eyes. I'd seen those eyes before and I've see them since, the eyes of a mother being brave in front of her kid; the universal eyes of the victim making the best of it. 'There are more important things to fight for than a bloody country,' she said. 'And I should know, my whole family has been sacrificed for one.' We were too young to understand sacrifice, for sacrifice without fear is no loss. We feared nothing and had even less to lose, we were virgins to a man. The door slammed in the face of our idealism.

In the stillness, the sound of two hundred TVs creamed in unison over Di's Emanuel wedding dress; it had more fabric in it than a camel train, and a train longer than the platform at Ponty, and that's the longest platform in Britain apparently. As if anybody cared.

'Can I help you boys?' Five heads turned to face Cliff, he was half way across the road and heading straight for us. Back of a bus for a face, he eclipsed the sun. 'What are you lot doing here then?' Jez mumbled, 'Nothing.' Cliff raised his finger and clicked, 'Oi, less of the lip sonny Jim, we don't want smart Alecs round 'ere right. Any trouble, I sort it out. Got it?' We nodded like five dachshunds in the back of an Escort.

'Now get back in your Mini and bugger... off.' He was face to face with Jez, or as near as damn to it, with a yard of gut in between. 'Vamoose kid,' he said, 'Don't let me catch your ugly face round here again!' By now the whole street was out on its doorstep staring at us; measuring us up, like antibody and virus.

The Valleys are tribal; streets are countries; districts, Empires. You're not a Rhondda lad, a Porth boy or a Glynfach kid, you're from Kimberly Way or Cymmer Road. Identity changes from street to street, like species in a rain forest. You live in a world as small as a Goldcrest's egg, and you protect your own whatever the price, and the price is always violent. Violence is the Valleys' lingua franca; the dialogue of the afraid wanting to instil fear.

Once, I met a warrior of eleven walking home; Mickey Mouse on his T shirt and an axe in his hand. I was eight and in awe. 'Where've you been?' I asked. 'Britannia,' he said. 'It was a hard fight. But in the end, we won.' I mumbled something about the honour of the street, 'That's right, kid,' he said and hobbled on.

By the time I carried the street's honour, standards had dropped. I remember when the gang went over to Penrhiwcoedcae Ponds and we caught the Tump kids sailing a dinghy amongst the sticklebacks. We were behind enemy lines, but they were slightly younger, so we took our chances, stole their dinghy and burnt it.

Two hours later, their big brothers ran into our street screaming revenge with pointy sticks; it was a scene out of a Laverbread Western. The Tump gang were in town and we were cowering behind curtains afraid to face them. There was bad blood between The Tump and The Dormas from that day on, a blood feud that will never be resolved until the Valleys flatten.

The Mini stalled, it was Fifi's car, but Fifi wasn't used to it, he'd only passed his test the week before. I had visions of a Mississippi style lynching. 'For God's sake Fifi. Get going!' Cliff's eyes burned through the car like sun dots on paper.

The plugs sparked, Fifi jammed the gears into first, balanced the pressure on his feet and we crawled away from the kerb like a dysentery patient out of the sun, barely gathering enough momentum to clear the end of the street. I closed my eyes in case we didn't make it.

In silence, we beat a retreat back down the Valley, back to a land that time hadn't quite forgotten. I opened my eyes around Abercarn, pressed my forehead against the back window, looked up at the mountain, and longed to walk its pine green carpet into the sun.

The summer before my father died, we climbed Snowdon. We climbed it with another father and his son. I forget the son's name, but our parting promise to each other was, when we grew up, I would build bridges and he would build ships to sail under them.
We took the Llanberis path, the easiest route, and stopped high above the tree line in the corrugated cafe. There we sipped tea from cracked china halfway between the Empire and the Valley; a quick breather before setting off for the peak. At first, the sky was clear, but two thirds of the way up, the cloud came down; still we climbed on, enveloped in a diffused grey light.

To keep us going, my father told a story about a man who went to a monastery on a week's retreat. He asked for an apple, a knife, a loaf of bread and to be locked in a cell for a week. Each night a monk stood outside the cell door to check if the man was all right, and each night he heard a strange sound coming from within. At the end of the week, the monk unlocked the cell door and the man stepped out. He offered no explanation for the sound, just made a date for the following year and left.

For twenty years the same thing happened, I know because we were treated to each year as we climbed. By the twenty-first year, the monk was due to retire, so it would be his last chance to confront the man.

As per every other year, the man arrived, asked for an apple, a knife, a loaf of bread and to be locked in a cell for the week. And each night, the monk stood outside the cell door and heard the familiar sound coming from within. At the end of the week, as it was the monk's last chance, when he opened the cell door, he picked up his courage and asked the man 'What was the sound?'… The man thought a while, handed back the knife, then told him. But what his answer was, my father refused to say; he left too much unsaid.

When we reached the peak, we headed straight for the cairn. And as my father lifted me onto the crown of Snowdon, there was a window in the cloud and the whole of Gwynedd appeared beneath me like a split Tesco bag spewing its contents around my feet. In my father's arms, I stood on top of the world. Within a year he was dead.

Fifi's Mini crawled asthmatically up the mountain road, pausing for the odd breather before resuming its climb. Like an Olympic torch carrier, staggering up the final few steps, it was about to ignite hope with not one, but five flames of burning ambition.

It had been a long journey to the top. For me, it started the first day I went to school and wet my pants coming home on the bus; a vague memory of being curled up on a teachers lap, pulling into Porth Square by the Post Office.

Welsh school was always a bus ride away: a double decker expedition through a Valley full of prejudice. Each school day was a journey towards a vision, we were too young to share the dream, but we were the realisation of its grand design. Like rare species in Jersey zoo, we were baby dragons, and each baby dragon was an integral part in the conservation plan.

We were pedigree, even the runts were spoon-fed in case they developed at a later date. We were special and we knew it, and this knowledge separated us from the 'English' kids in the Valley who stabbed us with their monoglot disgust: 'Bloody Welshie Bastards!' they'd shout at us.

But their words couldn't pierce the feeling of otherness which we wrapped around us like a protective skin. Dull wits don't scratch lead. What hope did they have of touching gold? We were precious, polished to catch the sun, trained in the art of of linguistic subversion.

I remember one school trip, we went to Tenby. I must have been about eight, the year before my father died. Fifty of us kids crammed in a shelter for the afternoon, whipping each other with cow parsley and boredom; outside, the rain whipped the waves into submission.

We'd all bought three things that day; pink rock, snowstorms and dragon tongues. The pink rock we sucked to points so fine even angels couldn't dance on them, the snowstorms we shook until they bled, and the dragon's tongues we bought because we were told to buy them and we did so without question.

It was a case of 'the teacher's apple', we all bought the badges of nationalism to please him; his preferences were our politics; his thought, our opinion. He taught us that Wales was its language, and the language was Wales. He led us to believe that the only true Welshman was the one who spat in the eye of oppression, naturally we wanted to spit with the best of them. So we spat over each other, spat over everything and we believed that through spitting we would all be a part of a glorious Welsh nation.

Unfortunately, as I grew older, I came to realise that not all spit is equal in Wales. There's an invisible spitting league and my brand of spit was in the relegation zone of the bottom division. My Welsh wasn't a mother tongue, it wasn't suckled from my mam's breasts in the pews of Capel Salem.

My accent was cooked up in the saucepan schools of the South East Wales; a blackboard exercise, unidiomatic and thin, the offspring of a marriage between a language and a region that had long since forgotten the sound of its own past.

My Welsh was a bastard, and by the age of fourteen, I realised that whilst one half of Wales giggled when I was spoke, the other half winced with pain at my cavalier use of mutation. It was a case of pedigree and I spoke with a mongrel tongue. I felt angry and defeated, rejected by a Frankenstein who balked at the monster he'd created.

It was around this time that I began staying regularly with Jez and his family. Without them I would have stopped speaking Welsh entirely and turned my back on the whole Welsh thing, but they pulled me back from the brink of Anglicisation.

They had a more laissez faire attitude towards the language. In school, it was a collar two sizes too small; with them, it was a sweat shirt, unrestrictive and comfortable. In their house Welsh wasn't the sole reason for communication, it was only the medium through which we conversed. They gave me the licence to duck and dive between languages and express myself without criticism, I was accepted for what I said, irrespective of idiom. In their house, Welsh was not the single issue, it was only one strand in a broader politic.

By the time we arrived at the picnic, the sansculottes had already gathered and claimed the mountain in the name of the Republic. Citizens had parked their Volvos, unpacked the bara brith and were in the process of buttering it.

Before I arrived, I had visions of Royalists being beheaded behind the barricades, there were only barbecues smouldering behind windjammers; big stripy things which looked as if they were on loan from Trecco Bay for the day.

Superficially, a change of flag, a bit less Laura Ashley, and the picnic would have been indistinguishable from any street party happening in the Valley below.

But beneath the surface, the difference was the discussion; talk of bombs and Nationalism, Welsh cakes and Socialism, Democracy and Darjeeling tea. Ideas and ideals tangoed together in the sun, Utopia danced a solo in the ballroom of my imagination. On that mountain top, I was given a glimpse of a broader horizon and I knew then that I would never climb back down, I had left the Valley for good. That knowledge made me feel both excited and guilty.

I thought about my mother in the Valley below. I imagined that she was dancing with some rat-arsed neighbour whilst my step father was probably dancing his hands all over the neighbour's wife. Shit like that happens whenever there's a Great British occasion; a Royal wedding or a football victory. It's always the way, the 'Dancing Dog Syndrome': give a Brit a bone and he'll dance all bloody day.

And by the sound of music vibrating the Valley walls, streets full of people were gyrating from Cwmparc to Cwmbran; dancing the Bacchanalian grope of the Royal Wedding.

For a second, I hovered on an hiatus of indecision. I was on the verge of swooping down into The Valley to reclaim the womb in my father's name. I wanted to protect my mother from all the fat nobodies who lusted after the cradle of my creation, but I was checked by the memory of something that happened when I was a kid.

One afternoon, whilst picking blackberries on the bank, I captured a Queen ladybird; a huge thing. I found an old match box, popped the ladybird in and ran home to show my mam. First she thanked me, then she opened the matchbox and shook it, 'Fly,' she said, freeing the ladybird. 'Never trap anything, or be trapped by anything, love,' she said, wiping the tears from my cheeks. Through a veil of tears my mother had watched the bus pull away for my first day at school; her tears had been a gift - the gift of freedom. Somehow, I felt sure that she hadn't put me on that bus to dance in the Valley, she had put me on that bus so that one day I could dance in the sun, and on that mountain top I was dancing. As I danced my guilt away, I knew that I would never pas de deux in Charmonds or dance the dance of the blunt fist in Wattstown ever again. I had danced out of darkness and into the light; danced like sherbet on the tongue and having danced once in the light, I vowed never to dance in the dark again. I telegraphed a thank you for my mother upon the wind and re-joined the conversation. 'No I didn't know the difference between Patriotism and Jingoism...'
Later that evening, Fifi's Mini rolled back down the mountain. Inside, at least one patriot, flaming with hope and rebellion, was about to hit reality with a bump.

The chicken stump stood on the lip of a trench. There, we built our home, marking it out with sticks; the outline of our little lives left open to the wind and our imagination. I was Tony Curtis, she was my kiss chase darling.

She would pulp the chicken stump with a stone until she'd carved enough flesh to feed her Viking when I returned home from the wars, walking the oars on a playground fjord.

One day, to celebrate a great victory, I stood on the lip of the trench, and jumped onto a breath of wind which carried me across the terraces to the other side of the Valley.

VOICEOVER

Way above Stanleytown, I banked to the left and followed the line of the mountain past Tylerstown and the Jubilee, past the still smouldering tip and on to Ferndale, which reclined dead ahead of me in terminal decay. Just before it I cut across the Valley floor and made a bee-line for the bars of Hendrefadog Spar. From there, I followed the Beirut roads to Penrhys Hill.

Just down from Mrs Humphreys' shop, I crossed into Bryn Terrace, swooped low over the iron bridge and banked to the left before the rugby field. Beneath me lay my junior school. I swooped down, hugging the hill, like a stealth jet navigating by sheep tracks. Just before the school railings, where once a dirty man touched girls through the bars, I pulled back and flew into the sun.

I rose til I felt the wax melt in my ears. Then I hung in the sky like a chucked stone motionless for an instant before it drops; a split second of absolute being before succumbing to gravity and coming down to earth once more. Then I dropped, like a faux pas in a dead party.

MAN

I landed at the bottom of the trench just five feet below the chicken stump. I had flown barely a second in real time, but I knew that even a second's flight is better than never flying.

On the night of the Royal Wedding, The Valleys leeched the National Grid, sucking the very last kilowatt out of the occasion; each village flamed, the whole Valley blazed like Swansea in the blitz. It was a night of electrifying excess after a day of over indulgence.

Rubbish lay strewn like confetti after a forgotten wedding, and drunks either lay for dead or wove patterns on pavements as they made their ways home to their graves for the night. Waste was everywhere and everyone was wasted.

I arrived home on my motorbike about ten; the house was a black hole in a universe of illumination. My mother and 'Him' were still out and I didn't have a key, I wasn't allowed to have one, not after the night when I arrived home at three in the morning. I spent a quarter of an hour struggling with the lock before realising that 'He'd' been standing the other side of the door, and he'd bolted it. When he eventually let me in, he said, 'Let me have a look at your key?' I gave it to him, he took it, turned it a few times in the lock and said 'There's nothing wrong with this key, kid, and by the way, you'll never have a key for this door again,' and that was that. Being keyless, I could've broken in, but somehow it didn't seem right on the night of the Royal Wedding. Instead, I parked my motorbike in the garage and walked to Wendy's.

Wendy wasn't a girlfriend in the top and bottom sense, but she had once made me immortal with her kiss; Bob Marley was 'Jamming' on the record player and there was a hint of Strawberry gateau on her lips. After that, I had high hopes, but she must have had a low opinion because we never kissed again. On the night of the Royal Wedding, I knew that her dad had declared an open house, so I grabbed the excuse to be near her.

'Cartref' was typically terraced with a flamboyant back extension; dressed up in MFI and bejewelled with lead crystal and little shields that had paper knives stuck in them. It was a comfortable house where feet were allowed to be put up and a lounge was where you lounged in. The family drove Escorts, ate chips without stigma and went to Spain at least once a year; a Utopia of sorts.

When I arrived, their mock mahogany front door was on the latch. I knocked all the same. 'We're in by here! Come in mun!' It was her father voice, the butcher; his finger nails always looked as if he had flesh under them; the perfume of death clung to him. 'Alex, boy, hate to tell you, but you've just missed Wendy. Everybody's popped off to a party in Banog see. Have a seat though, she might be back in a bit. Fancy a beer kid?'

I nodded and perched awkwardly on a wing. 'Make yourself comfortable mun.' He pushed a Colt 45 into my hand, I thanked him, and slipped into the chair. 'There, that's better,' he said.

'How are you love?' White teeth, marbled eyes, the butcher's wife sat across her stockinged heels. 'We didn't see you in the street party this afternoon. Saw your mam though, she was with your dad.' 'He's not my father,' I said, killing the conversation dead.

The butcher's dog rolled over in the silence. The butcher's wife's took a sip of gin and a drop hung from her lower lip. 'Still, nothing like a wedding or a funeral to bring people together, is there?' she said, catching the droplet in a sharp breath. I stood up 'Don't shoot off straight away love, you've hardly touched your beer. Do you want a glass for it?'
She smiled, I smiled, the butcher burped. 'Pardon me,' he said. 'So where've you been quoting all day then?' He listened as I told him

about the picnic; eyes glazed, he nodded in all the right places. 'That's nice for you kid.'

'Shame,' his wife interjected, ''cause you missed a lovely day today, didn't he love? Princess Diana looked gorgeous in her wedding dress, made by a Welshman it was, and there was Welsh gold in her wedding ring. Makes you proud to be Welsh, don't it darling?' 'Damn right it does.' 'Diana looked lovely, Alex. Not a patch on our Wendy though, don't you think so?' She searched my eyes for a reaction, they played dead. 'You like our Wendy don't you, Alex?'

I smiled numbly. 'Wendy told us, we're very close as a family, we share everything, see. You like her a lot don't you, love? We like her a lot as well. Don't we Phil?' 'Goes without saying.' The butcher's wife raised her eyebrows and reached for the gin, 'Tell him then.' 'Tell him what, love?' 'You know,' she said, 'about what we talked about'. 'Oh that,' he said, sidling from rump to rump.

The butcher sharpened his breath as he would a knife before slicing lamb. 'The thing is, right,' he began, 'and I'm not saying this behind Wendy's back, because it's what she said to us but she hasn't got the heart to say to you. She doesn't want to hurt your feelings see, and neither do we. Are you all right for beer, kid?' His wife cut in, 'Phil love, spit it out, the boy's got to know sooner or later.' 'Hold the boat love, it's not easy to say this. See Alex, it's not that she doesn't like you, she thinks a lot of you. It's just that you're different to her and she feels uncomfortable with that. You talk about things she doesn't understand. Now, I'm not doing her down, because she's my daughter and I only want the best for her, but Wendy is simpler than you, I don't mean twp simple, I mean, she's different to you, you know what I mean. Wendy thinks that you're a nice boy Alex, but the thing is'… he paused, and his wife brought the cleaver down,

'... It's the Welsh, love. Now don't get me wrong, it's great that you go to Welsh school and all that, I wish I spoke the language myself, but I don't, and neither does Wendy and that makes a world of difference, see.' I didn't see, but I suppose I wasn't looking.

At that moment Wendy burst in, her arms wound around a boy who was destined to develop labourer's crack. 'All right Mr Vallence,' he said, muscles in his voice. 'Right as rain, son,' the butcher emphasised the word 'son'. 'Nice to see you Robert, you know you're always welcome.'

Eyes on stalks, the butcher's wife thought, 'If only I was twenty again, I'd submit myself to a second submission.' Instead, she pursed her passion and asked, 'Wasn't the party good then love?' 'Dead as Dinas mam...' Wendy cawed, her beauty and her voice in inverse proportion '... more life in a crem'. She turned and gave me the once over. 'What are you doing here?' she asked. The eyes of the Valley demanded an answer, I didn't have one.

'I've got to go,' I said, standing up and spilling my can of beer. 'Don't worry about it, love, it'll match the carpet pattern,' the butcher's wife patronised me with priggish eyes. Wendy's eyes said much more, they joined forces with Gary's grin and annihilated my ego. The butcher chipped in. 'You know your way out, don't you kid. Nice to see you kid. Give my regards to your mother, tell 'er she dances a lovely tango.'

As I went for the door, I passed through a cloud of Wendy's perfume: Anais Anais, the memory of an outstretched neck and our only kiss. 'See you then Alex,' she said dismissing an unwelcome guest. Not even a 'We must do this again' and a smile upon her lips. Just 'See you then Alex'.

When I arrived home, the house was still dark. I climbed onto the flat roof, manoeuvred onto the dormer and made my way across the tiles, clinging to the window sills for balance. At my bedroom window, I flipped open the catch and broke in, squeezing my body through an eighteen-by-nine opening. I undressed in the dark, lay down on my bed and let my thoughts wander the mountain.

Twenty years passed before I climbed Snowdon again. As a child, I had climbed free at my father's side; as an adult, I climbed with a heavy heart and a heavy pack. After postcards from the peak, to prove I had been there, I was faced with a choice. I either slid back down the way I had climbed up, or took a different path. I chose Crib Goch, and that made all the difference.

After the crocodile smile of the first few hundred yards, I saw before me the lower jaw of a carnivore who files his teeth upon the wind. Its grin was a gauntlet slap in the face of dignity.

In the safety of the Valley, I had preached that there is no past, no present and no future, there is only 'It'. I realised that this was 'It'; the moment I had only pontificated about. On that mountain, for the first time in my journey towards death, I realised that I was on the verge of living. So gathering all time and vertigo into my backpack, I faced the challenge and walked on.

The ridge was barely a foot wide. On my left, the mountain dropped vertically to oblivion. On my right, there was an eighty degree gradient. Immediately I sank on all fours and crawled crabwise across the face. Pressing nose to rock, my eyes studied the shape of each stone as my hands searched beyond me for a grip. All the while, my backpack threatened to over balance me and drag me to my death. I had visions of being dismembered like a car off a cliff.

Inch by inch, I traversed the rock, trying desperately to avoid nearing the top of the ridge. At one point, I had no choice, I couldn't find any hand or foot holds, so I had to climb up to the edge. Peering over, I saw people hang-gliding beneath me!

First I froze, then I scrambled down a few feet, turned foetus and shook.

After a while, all fear dissolved and I embraced an absolute tranquillity; the calmness of ultimate terror; the ecstasy of saints. I stopped shaking and reasoned that my only course of action was to jump off the mountain and fly.

On Crib Goch, after making peace with my world, I was on the verge of sailing the wind when I saw a man walk the ridge above me. He didn't crawl on all fours across the face, he walked, knowing the danger, embracing the fear.

Suddenly, I felt imbued with a passion for life; the desire to keep living. I realised that I had to walk that blade's edge off that mountain. So I grasped the wind in my palms, stood on the ridge, and walked the mountain's teeth into the sun.

By the time they came home, I was asleep. I was woken up by 'His' scream as he raised the dead then tried to deafened them. 'Who the fuck put that chair there?' 'You did, Andrew.' 'Oh fuck it.' 'Sh! You'll wake the neighbours,' my mother said. 'I don't care who I bloody wake, I've hurt my bloody leg mun. You're lucky it's not bloody bleeding.' 'Alex is probably asleep, Andrew.' 'So, the little bugger's come home, has he? Come home have you boy?' His voice straddled the banister and invaded my bed. 'Had a nice time with all your Welshie friends, have you kid?' 'For God's sake Andrew, don't be inconsiderate.' 'I'll inconsider who the hell I bloody well like, it's a free country isn't it? To be inconsiderate is a British right, my father fought a bloody war to be inconsiderate. Are you listening kid?'

He began to climb the stairs. The last time the stairs lay between us, he was at the top, I was at the bottom, I'd superglued his tape deck and he wanted to teach me a lesson. He stood thirteen steps above me and commanded, 'Come here and accept your punishment like a man.' Slowly I climbed the stairs towards him; it was the highest mountain I have ever climbed, either before or since then.

As I reached the third stair, he reached for his buckle and undid his belt. 'Shift your arse, I haven't got all day, kid!' At the seventh stair, his belt hung flaccid in his hand. Eighth, ninth; a child walked towards a man, but the man was too much of a child to forgive him. When I reached the thirteenth stair, he grabbed me by my arm, folded me over the banister and thrashed his own inadequacy out on my backside. 'I'll tan your hide,' he squealed as the leather bit in, 'I've had a guts-full of your ruddy shenanegans.'
'No trouble now Andrew,' my mother said at the top of the stairs, 'You're drunk and you don't know what you're doing.' 'I know what I'm doing. Don't tell me I'm drunk when I'm not bloody drunk woman!'

I knew 'His' anger when I heard it; the din of a toddler hammering a piano with its fists. But that night, I sensed something darker in his tone; something sinister. I got out of bed and waited for the shit to hit the fan: without the shit it wouldn't have been a great British occasion.

The bedroom door framed his approach. 'To what do we owe this honour, then kid?' 'Come on Andrew, let's go to bed.' 'I'm not going to bed yet!' His breathing was heavy, his steps deliberate. He swayed in the pub atmosphere he'd brought home with him; sweet on his breath, stale on his shirt.

'You missed a great day today, didn't he love? Everybody had a good time, didn't they love? Everybody had a good time, that is, apart from us. We were too embarrassed to enjoy it kid. Everybody kept asking us, 'Where's Alex?' Graham and Barbara, Alan and Doreen, the whole bloody street kept asking, 'Where is he?' What the hell were we supposed to say eh? That you were on a fascist picnic? His nibs was lording it up on top of an hill with all his Welshie friends 'cause his family are not good enough for him? Your mother was ashamed, kid. Ashamed! And don't say you weren't love 'cause I saw your face. You were embarrassed, and I was embarrassed for you, as embarrassed as fuck!'

He was always embarrassed as fuck; tired as fuck, happy as fuck. Fuck must have been a God in his pantheon, because every time 'He' was exasperated 'He' invoked Fuck's name.'For fuck's sake kid, look at me when I'm talking to you! Look at me kid!'

When things pass a certain point, you know something's going to blow, like the line they've calculated for species extinction; one whale over the line and the whole damn lot go. As soon as 'He' stepped over the door frame, I retreated to the furthest point in my skull, putting as much distance as possible between my senses and the man who was assaulting them. 'What the hell do you think you're playing at? Uh? What the hell do you think you're playing at? Are you bloody stupid or what? Are you going to apologise to your mother? What have you got to say for yourself then? Uh? Uh!' The only thing I wanted to say was 'Just fucking Go!' It came out as 'The butcher asked me to tell mam, she dances a lovely tango.'

'You what…!' 'The butcher…' 'I fucking heard what you said, you little bastard.' He started poking my chest with straight fingers as if he was conducting a symphony in staccato. 'You stupid… stupid… stupid bastard.' My mother grabbed his arm 'Let me go woman, it's about time someone taught your son a fucking lesson.'

The lesson began when his fist landed in my face. My neck hinged, and my head echoed to the sound of drum sides being hit by a hammer.

112

Then like a rat, he went for my neck. His arm swung round my shoulder as if he was welcoming a friend, but it didn't stop at the far side, it continued its movement round until he held my neck in a tight grip.Then he twisted me down and manoeuvred me under his arm pit. As 'He' squeezed, I felt the pressure build up behind my eyes. I closed them tight to keep them in.

On a screen of stars, I saw one Saturday afternoon when I was watching wrestling with my gran. A wrestler squeezed a man's neck 'til he fell unconscious in front of millions on live TV; almost a snuff movie. If they hadn't brought him round within a minute he would've been brain dead; everyone knew the risk, but no-one stopped the fight.

I kissed another fist. 'I'm going to fucking kill you,' he said, 'You and your fucking language. You Welsh git!' My mother screamed the wallpaper from the walls 'Stop it, Andrew. Can't you see what you're doing?' 'I know what I'm bloody doing,' he said 'I'm just trying to help him see what he's fucking done. But he doesn't want to see further than his fucking nose. Well if he wants to see fuck all, lets see how he sees when I rip his fucking eyes out.'

I felt fingers fumble my face, Oedipus trying to blind Oedipus. My mother tried to scream a wedge between us. She pulled his fingers away from my eyes. He crowed a laugh, but I didn't see the funny side of his fist. Wham! He repeated the joke, then joked some more. Wham! Wham! Have you heard the one about a Welshie, a Paki and a Queer? Wham! Wham! Wham!

Even though he was hurting me, I made no effort to free myself from his grip, I allowed him to stamp his impotence upon my face, realising that each blow hurt my mother much more than it could ever hurt me. I conceded the battle for the sake of overall victory.

'Please stop it Andrew,' my mother pounded her final plea upon his back, 'Why are you doing this?' 'I'm teaching him a lesson he'll never forget. The little git's ruining this family with his fucking selfishness!' 'What's there to ruin?' My mother screamed. 'You've already ruined everything and killed us dead!' Silence. In the silence lay his defeat. 'Fuck you!' he forced through tight lips. Stillness, as he considered what to do next. I could smell the confusion in his sweat. He manoeuvred me from under his armpit and held me in a standing head hold. Out of the corner of my eye, I saw a smile crawl across his gobby lips. 'Bastard,' he whispered, breathing his hate into my brain; twisting the knife one final time before releasing me.

'He' avoided my mother's eyes as he brushed past her onto the landing, but I saw them. I saw a prayer for the dead welling up within, I saw her pain and I swear I heard the sobs of a dead man crying. 'I'm sorry Alex,' my mother said, there was no need for her to say sorry, but she did. Then she turned and closed my bedroom door behind her as she left.

I left the way I had come in. Quietly, I slipped through the window, unlocked the garage door and wheeled my motorbike to the top of the drive. 'Alex,' my mother shouted as I kick started the engine; first gear, clutch out, throttle back and I was flying; past cars, past caring. Flying to Ponty and beyond; like leaping off a bloody mountain.

I flew through the night, star hopping, stopping only to refuel on the dark side of the moon.

When I got home the next morning, I stood at the bottom of the stairs and 'He' walked down the stairs towards me. He carried a suitcase in each hand. 'I'm leaving. It's probably for the best, eh kid? Look, I'm really sorry about last night. I know I was way out of order but the thing is…' He put his bags down and held out his hand. 'Sorry. What do you say, do you forgive me?' Silence. 'I can understand you,' I said 'but I can never forgive.' Then, leaving him at the bottom of the stairs, I climbed to the top of the highest mountain and soared into the sun.

VOICEOVER

In time, I was to climb out of the Valley. In time, I shall return to it as dust; an handful of unanswered question thrown into the sun's eye from the top of a mountain. For the valley is a funnel with greased lips, the pain of a million Sisyphuses'. Born in the valley, we can never truly escape it, though we may rise to the brim and glimpse freedom promised in a beam of light, we are allowed only instants of hope before sliding back under the weight of our legacy, back into the pit where all pits have been and gone. But still we climb on, because in our moments of light lie our reasons for living.

Roger Williams has written plays for theatre companies including Made In Wales and The Sherman Theatre Company; television for BBC2, HTV and S4C; and radio for BBC Radio Wales and BBC Radio Cymru. His plays include *Gulp, Surfing Carmarthen Bay* and *Killing Kangaroos*. In 1998-99 he was playwright-in-residence at Sydney Theatre Company and the Australian National Playwrights' Centre. In 2000 he was awarded a Playwright's Bursary by the Arts Council of Wales. He lives in West Wales.

Saturday Night Forever

Roger Williams

Lee - **Sean Carlsen**
Director - **Steven Fisher**
Designer - **Carolyn Willitts**
Technical Design - **Simon Wheatley**
Assistant Director - **Alex Alderton**

First performed at Chapter Arts Centre, Cardiff, July 1998, by
cf1.theatre.com, and subsequently at The Edinburgh International
Fringe Festival. This version produced by The Sherman Theatre
Company in March 2001 in Cardiff and on tour.

Darkness

VOICE

No. Don't. I'm begging you, don't. Please! Fuck. Don't do this. No! No! Don't. Fuck! Don't!

Dance music pounds from the speakers, grows louder, until it drowns out the voice. Lights blaze. Lee enters carrying a bottle of beer. He is in his early twenties, tall, attractive, and dressed as though out at a club. He scans the room, watches the audience, and comes forward. The music stops, the lights steady, and Lee turns to address the audience.

LEE

Saturday night started at one o'clock. At least that's when it started for Matthew. One o'clock, Saturday afternoon.

You'd be lucky to get a word out of him before the credits had rolled on *CD:UK*, and he'd had at least three fags and a Fuse bar. But when the boybands stopped miming, and ITV geared up for Formula One, Matthew'd yawn wide, fight the lure of the sofa, adjust his boxer shorts, and announce, 'I'm gonna get ready. Five minutes alright?'

And half-an-hour later he'd be back. Emerging from the steam of the bathroom like a contestant appearing through the dry ice of *Stars In Their Eyes*. Transformed, smiling, and ready for anything. He'd check that his Visa card and fringe were safely in place before scouring the house for his fugitive door keys, and pulling on a jacket. Saturday night was coming, and in order to make the most of it, Matthew had to start early.

You see, in Matthew's world, Saturday nights were important. Too important to pass by without some sort of celebration or event. Saturday nights, like lazy days, summer holidays, and Belgian chocolates, were meant to be enjoyed. He looked forward to them all week long, getting more and more excited as he counted the days go by; an expectant child working his way through an advent calendar.

He loved the ritual of dressing up and going out. Drinking, laughing, and dancing until the CDs were tired of spinning. It was his religion, and like other true believers Matthew had to prepare for it. After all, Saturday nights only came round once a week and you had to make the most of them; they were precious. Procedures had to be adhered to, questions asked, and decisions made. Where? When? And probably most importantly: 'What on earth am I going to wear?'

The first two questions were easily answered with one quick call to a fellow worshipper. 'The Kings, half-eight. See ya there.' But the remaining problem was more of a challenge. And after rifling through an overworked wardrobe that was near to bursting, he'd give up, and decide emergency action had to be taken. In other words - he needed to go shopping.

Matthew was a pro, and would willingly spend all day Saturday searching the rails for something new to wear. Barker, Floyd, dodging the traffic to Westworld. He looked for something loud and different. French Connection, Gap. Something garish, or see-through, that could only ever be worn in the shadows of a night-club, where the fashion police weren't on patrol and everyone else was too drunk to care. He wanted a clubber's uniform; something that said to everyone else in the room, 'Hey! Look at me! I'm having a fabulous time, and I'm wearing the trousers to prove it!'

Matthew was scrupulous in his selection. And it was only when he had found something special, and believe me, he could always find something special, that he'd relax and agree to go home. Chuffed to bits, he'd sit on the back seat of the bus grinning gormlessly like a big kid; satisfied, complete. In a world of his own, he'd be privately mixing and matching every pair of trousers he already owned with the shirt he'd just bought. Saturday night was coming and he was planning his look. A place just left of heaven. 'Tonight's going to be brilliant,' he'd whisper, before deciding whether he wanted fish-fingers or spaghetti for tea.

Matthew dropped anchor in front of the television as soon as he got back. Surrounded by his new purchases he'd loll before the screen armed with the remote control and a copy of *TV Quick*. Lazing happily on an imaginary lilo, adrift in a sea of carrier bags, he'd stare in awe as John Virgo made another *Big Break* and Cilla Black made more matches in hell. Transfixed. Lost somewhere on the road between Holby City and Jonathan Creek he'd be going through the motions of a Saturday night in his head. Praying that everything went to plan. It was only of course when Martin and Marie had torn one another to shreds after a nightmare all-expenses-paid-for blind date in the Seychelles, that he'd stir and start to get changed.

Every so often though he'd panic and appear in the corridor semi-dressed with a mouthful of questions. 'What d'you reckon? Is this shirt too tight? Do these trousers make my arse look big? What'll I do with my hair?' And his friends'd give answers that were always ignored because, not answering to the name of Donna Karan, they obviously didn't know what the hell they were talking about. But they tried. 'Yes too tight.' 'What arse?' and 'Oh, just cut it all off!'

Miraculously, as the cab was pulling up outside, he'd saunter into the hall with every single hair on his head suffocated in a layer of thick gel, and the shirt he'd bought earlier that afternoon gripped to his chest like cling-film. 'Right,' he'd declare, 'Ready. And I'll tell you something for nothing, I'm going to get hammered tonight.'

A few drinks here-and-there later; Bar Cuba, Ha-Ha's, Matthew'd inevitably make his final pilgrimage to the same old club, where he'd have one drink too many and motor around the dance floor like a Weeble that won't fall down. He'd wail along to Madonna, sashay to Kylie, and stand still, cross armed, refusing to dance another step in protest, when the DJ dared to play anything half-decent. I.e. something with a guitar in it.

Matthew loved Saturday night, and I hated him for it. I hated the way he gossiped bitchily with his pack of friends at the bar, flirted with strangers, and drank Diamond White suggestively from its bottle. Always the same game. I could guarantee you that by the end of the night, he'd be pig drunk, would've snorted speed like a vaccuum cleaner, and jumped up on stage to mime the part of Agnetha when the DJ played *Voulez Vous*.

So it was, to say the least then, a bit of a problem that Matthew was my boyfriend, and that we'd been seeing each other for six months.

I didn't play his games. We were fundamentally different. While he hit the dance-floor looking for laughs, I took up a defensive position at the bar. But I didn't dance. Never. I just don't. I'm one of those people you see in night clubs standing at the edge of the dance-floor watching everyone else let go. One of those people you find looking on. Allergic to rhythm.

I make an effort of course. I mouth the lyrics like a goldfish, tap my foot to the beat, and sway back and forth just to show willing. A spectator at a football match I'll never be good enough to play in. I could never star in the Premier League like Matthew.

Nobody in my family can dance. It's hereditary. Like the colour of your eyes or the size of your feet. At the school disco in 1985 I found out the hard way that the dreaded gene had been passed on to me in my DNA. And as *Wake Me Up Before You Go Go* bled from the sound system, I died on the dance-floor surrounded by my so called mates, who gawped, stared, and pointed. Shot down by the laughter of cruel teenagers I quickly accepted that some people simply weren't built to dance. And soon after Andrea Morgan's public admonishment that I was, 'An embarrassment!' who, 'Should've stayed home with the rest of the saddos!' I gave up, and learnt to deliver a firm 'no' when anyone suggested heading towards the music.

I discovered mountains of excuses as I trekked from party to pub, and disco to night-club, en route through the landscape of a Saturday night. 'Can't dance sorry, twisted my ankle playing rugby last night, and it really hurts, ow.' 'Just off to the bog, I'm dying for a piss. You go ahead, I'll catch you up.' Like Doctor David Banner I'd lurk in the shadows. 'Don't make me dance. You really wouldn't like me when I dance.'

So when Saturday night came round and we headed into town, I clung to the edge of the pool while everyone else splashed about in the deep end.

'So? You gonna dance with us tonight then mister or what?' Matthew asked when he was bored of playing with his new friends. The 'D' word. 'I was only asking. Don't know why some people are so touchy. It's not like anyone's looking at you now is it?'

Alright. Perhaps I should've kept my mouth shut. Perhaps I should've bitten my lip and ended the relationship if not gracefully, then at least sober. But I didn't. And instead, I snapped. As I watched Matthew revelling with his disciples under the blazing lights and buzz of the room I said it, and in doing so, broke his faith.

It was when Take That exploded from the speakers that it happened. Usually I wouldn't've minded, but having already endured The Spice Girls, Celine Dion, and Steps, I'd had enough. As soon as I heard Gary Barlow's deafening warble I could feel it building up inside me. The rage. The anger. The hatred against a record collection that needed burning.

No way back. Pushed off the ledge and falling faster than a body builder from a tenth floor window, I found myself turning to Matthew, just turning to him and saying, 'Take That are shit'.
'You what?' he asked, not quite hearing me I don't think over the music and cries of ecstasy that were flying up from the crowd.
'Take That are shit. I hate Take That.'
'Don't be so fucking soft,' he replied, gulping at his cider, and waving over at an ex-boyfriend who was drowning amid a flood of naked torsos.
'Nah. I mean it. I hate Take That. I really really hate them.'
'No you don't.'
'Fucking do! I'm glad they split up!'

And it was that comment that did it. Those five words. Harmless independently, but when strung together, a dangerous cocktail that struck at Matthew's nervous system like cyanide. He looked at me as if I'd plunged a knife deep into his chest, 'But, but, we like Take That.'
'No Matthew, you like Take That. You like Take That, the same as you like Hollyoaks, Titanic, Habitat, Malibu Breezers, and this fucking hole. I don't. I never have done.'
'Bollocks,' he responded.
'Yeah. It is isn't it?'

And as he called after me, I looked back at him and saw the little boy. Pitiful. Lost. I left before his tears could dry.

Music blares out: Take That 'Everything Changes'. It fades as before. Lee removes his coat.

LEE

Saturday nights 'in' were a cause that needed to be championed. Early nights, long phone calls with old friends, *Casualty*, I didn't know why people insisted going out at all. I mean, getting bladdered, copping off, having fun... Who needs it?

Once I would've been trekking up Mill Lane at nine o'clock on a Saturday, but now I was tucked up in bed watching the latest heart-throb Doctor in *Casualty* perform mouth-to-mouth on handsome patients. Wondering hopelessly whether there'd be a very long waiting list for that kind of treatment on the NHS. I took Saturday nights off. Allowed myself to be lazy. Kicked back. Unwound.

This was life after Matthew. And like a new pair of trainers, the novelty soon wore off. Like life without a telly or a vegetarian diet, self-imposed exile had drawbacks. I was missing the terrain of the social circuit. Frightened I was missing out. So when I heard that Emma was having a party at the weekend I grabbed it as a lifeline, 'When d'you want me?', and invited myself along.

Saturday came round and I ventured outside again with a bottle of Tesco's cheapest wedged under my arm and headed over to Riverside for salvation. It was dark. I'd forgotten what it was like to be out at this time on a weekend. Groups of friends on the way to the pub pushed past me pumped up for another big Saturday adventure. Excited. Primed. Men on a mission lumbered by with great expectations and even bigger imaginations.

'Hardly any point me goin' out tonight boys. Wait an' see, I'll be back home again by nine doing the business with some lucky young lady on the bedroom carpet.'

'Nine o'clock? Slow worker aren't you?'

'And I'll leave her in no doubt that heaven, contrary to popular opinion, is a place on earth.'

'Yeah, but I don't think anyone'll believe it's in Ely.'

And as they moved by in their Ben Sherman shirts and Calvin Klein jeans, laughing and shouting, I felt a little uneasy, scared. The geography was unfamiliar, foreign, and standing here as a stranger it struck me as volatile, unsafe.

Spice Girls in training were doing their bit for girl power in Max Factor colours and halter neck tops on Romilly Road. Wrapped up in small dresses that'd look 'Fab!' under the lights, they bared the cold wind in a cloud of thick hair-spray, and came out together for fun.
'Lindsey! Lindsey! You comin' out or what? It's half-past eight already an' I said we'd be there by quarter past! Never mind yer zits girl, they're not gonna be looking at yer face now are they!'
An animal out of hibernation my senses were heightened. I waited for something to explode, for one of the leery passers by to approach me, stop me, jeer me.
'We goin' down The Emporium, Jude? I loves it there.'
The stuff of dreams.

A car sped past me, its stereo growling, and the paranoia won over. 'Keep your head down. Low profile. Don't provoke anyone. You're alright. Keep walking. Keep moving. Just in case.'

The party was well under way by the time I arrived. Emma greeted me at the door, draped herself around my neck like a feather boa, and pinched my bum.
'Alright beautiful?' she croaked.
They'd been drinking since lunch time and I could feel the haze of alcohol rising on her breath like the steam from a boiling hot bath.

'Come on then? Where's my prezzie?' she demanded.
I presented her with the bottle of plonk and the birthday card I'd spent an hour choosing and five seconds writing. She led me through the hall and straight into the furnace of the celebrations.

'Hey Paula, this is the one I was telling you about!'

Paula, Emma's best mate, was wrapped up in some strange man's arms talking horoscopes and fiddling with his chest hair.

'The agoraphobic? Bless. He's quite cute isn't he?'

'Woha! Don't start getting ideas girl. He's no go. Dresses on the left.'

'You what?'

'Tt. Honest to God, you can be dull sometimes! He comes from planet poof!'

Alright, perhaps I am exaggerating, but I could've sworn that at that moment every head in the room turned three hundred and sixty degrees and looked at me. Freeze frame. The monkey boy. The man with three nipples. The ho-mo-sex-u-al.

'It's good to see you bach,' Emma wailed. 'Make yourself comfy. I'll be back in a sec. Just got to go and strangle whoever's playing this music. Shit, isn't it?' With which she fled in search of whoever'd loaded her CD player with *Mambo Number Five* and pressed 'repeat'.

I struggled to find a face I could recognise and latch onto. No joy. Watching so many socially adept people at work only made me feel like even more of an outsider. I didn't speak this language. Like a South Walian lost in Caernarfon, I didn't understand. 'You what?' I felt self-conscious, wanted Emma to come back and translate. The paranoia was kicking in. Norman-no-mates. Stranger in the corner. I considered the options. Go. Stay. Leave. Dissolve...

'You're Lee aren't you? I'm Carl. Emma's brother. You having a good time? I hate going to parties where I don't know anyone.'

A fellow traveller.

'You too? I'm glad I'm not the only one who feels like a total dick.'

'Well, no. I know most of the people here. I mean you. Emma said you haven't been going out that much lately.'

Bitch.

'Bad break up was it?'

Double bitch.

'I've been through something similar myself recently. Two months we were together.'

'Ah, right.'

The conversation lumbered to a halt. I couldn't think of anything sensible to say so I didn't. The music stopped. Emma must've won her battle with the stereo. I shuffled uncomfortably in my chair, trying to think of a way to jump start the conversation that wouldn't have sounded naff. Carl beat me to it. And taking my glass from my hand asked, 'Want a refill?'

And with that single shot of vodka the conversation took off and veered wildly from subject to subject like an out-of-control car being driven by a twelve-year-old. Everyone else in the house danced, copped off, and got high, while Carl and I had great discussions about everything that's important in life. Politics, culture, *Buffy the Vampire Slayer...*

Look, I know I promised myself it wouldn't happen again. I know I'd sworn that I wasn't going to, under any circumstance, go back to that place, that nightmare place I'd just escaped from, but, but, as we talked, and as I laughed, I think that for the first time since breaking up with Matthew, I actually started to fancy somebody.

Carl was a teacher. Carl came from Penarth. Carl had a degree in Sociology. Carl drank lager. Carl went to Ibiza for his holidays. Carl was gorgeous and I would've joined his fan club right there and then if he'd had one. He was tall, with cropped black hair, and a chiselled face that could've sold suits for Armani. So what was the problem? The problem was, as Carl told me at precisely four-thirty-three in the morning and after far too much booze, that he'd just split up with Debbie.

Ok, so I might've known deep down that my chances of getting past first base with this man were slim, but you've got to have hope haven't you? And the longer we'd talked the further I'd fallen, but the mention of Debbie crushed the castles I'd been building. He'd had a girlfriend. He was het-er-o-sex-u-al. He couldn't help it.

It was late and this last blow was too much. Carl was a nice man. We'd had a great conversation during which I'd deluded myself that we would've made a great couple. Somewhere in my fantasy world I'd even picked out a colour scheme for our living room. Burnt oranges and reds if you must know. But I didn't particularly want to sit around super gluing his broken ego back together. Especially since the incentive of a snog had been so cruelly snatched away from me. Carl was getting over a failed relationship. It was Sunday morning. Very early Sunday morning. I wanted a wee. I wanted to go home. What I didn't want to hear about was Debbie. So before he could go any further, I made an executive decision, stood up, and left.

As I stepped out onto a deserted Rolls Street I was bitten by the cold wind. I stuffed my hands down deep into my pockets and hunched myself up tight. 'Bloody heterosexuals. Get everywhere, don't they?' I hadn't gone far before Carl caught up with me.
'Hey, why d'you dash off like that? Did I say something wrong? Did I offend you?'
'No, I'm just tired.'
'We were getting on well weren't we? We were having a good time. I was telling you about Debbie. I thought you liked me.'
The white noise faded. Normal service resumed.
'Debbie broke up with me, because...' I could feel my hearting beating. 'Because...' Faster.
What?
'Because I told her that,' he waited, bit his lip, 'I told her I liked men. I mean, that I was, y'know, erm, gay, like.'

As impossible as it may seem now, this beautiful man I'd been chasing around inside my head all night had just come out to me. Standing in the middle of the street, barefoot, at something-hideous-past-four in the morning, this seemingly straight, football playing, lager drinking, Brit pop fan, who looked a bit like Man United's Michael Owen, had come out to me.

Carl stared wide eyed, puzzled, waiting for a reaction other than shock to cross my face. There was a gap where language froze in the cold morning air, and it seemed only right that at that surreal moment fire works should've gone off somewhere, that great big rockets should've screamed across the sky and burst open. Flashes of red, yellow, green. An orchestra should've started playing and Carl's family come running out of the surrounding houses to embrace him like a game-show winner, congratulated him for having the guts to tell the world, well, me at least, that he was gay. It didn't happen of course. It never does.

Carl looked down at his feet and waited for an answer. He shivered. I desperately wanted to say something that'd make it all better, make him feel alright. Say something clever and profound that'd put all his fears to rest. But all I could say at that particular moment was, 'Chilly, isn't it?' And he agreed that it was.

Music. It fades. Lee undoes a top shirt button, pulls his shirt out of his trousers and rolls up his sleeves.

LEE

We didn't do anything that night of course. We didn't! I mean, I didn't kiss him. Nor did I drag him back to my place, strip him naked, smear his thighs with golden syrup, and get down to some seriously sticky love making. No, I waited until the following weekend before I did that; before I stepped over the invisible line that separates attraction from action.

As I walked along Cathedral Road to keep the date we'd made my brain went into panic. Would Carl turn out to be Matthew mark two? Was there a disco queen lurking beneath his mild mannered exterior? Should I prepare myself for... But as I neared the pub and saw Carl standing outside waiting for me wearing a battered pair of jeans, trainers, and one of those hooded tops zipped half way up I knew I was doing the right thing. His hair was its usual scruffy self and when he saw me coming he raised a hand, sniffed and said, 'Alright?' From the size of the smile on my face I think he knew that it was.

Carl wasn't like Matthew. That's probably why I liked him. Carl listened. He wasn't hyperactive. Carl read the newspapers, and could sit through an entire film at the cinema without getting up to fetch popcorn. Carl didn't talk all the way through a good TV programme, didn't spend hours in front of a mirror, liked Blur, Pulp, Radiohead, and thought that Take That should've been aborted at twenty-eight weeks. Let's just say we had things in common.

Carl was one of those people you meet from time to time, talk to for a while, and by the end of the night, end up thinking, 'Fuck! I wish I was like that.' I wish I was as clever, good looking, eloquent, relaxed, and effortlessly fashionable as him. Bastard. He was the man your mother would've approved of. Even if your mother was one of those wicked dragons that'd threatened to disown you for having unnatural and unhealthy relations with men and their willies. It was official. Everyone liked him.

We walked slowly away from the pub after last orders and headed down Llandaff Road. The streets of Cardiff were sleeping, but as we turned the corner we very nearly walked into the middle of a fight. A sudden nightmare. Two men throwing punches. Shouting and swearing like nobody's business. Danger. One of them dropped his chips. 'Bastard! My curry sauce!' Carl reassuringly put an arm around my shoulder and steered me away.

'Here we are then.'

'Yeah, here we are.'

We were standing under a street light outside my house. I hunted for my door key. Carl waited. He wasn't going anywhere. Imagine a hideous pause as we watched one another trying to act casual under the lamp's hazy Swalec glow. Both freezing. Both longing to go inside. But both waiting for the other to suggest it first.

'Live here alone then, d'you?'

Opening question. Let's get the ball roling.

'With a couple of friends yeah.'

Friendly smile, casual response.

'It looks nice.'

And that was the comment I'd been waiting for which allowed me to go one stage further. I acted as though a sudden brain wave had just hit me, and spontaneously asked, 'Oh, well, do you want to come in and have a look round?' So alright, it wasn't that much further up the evolutionary scale than, 'Want to come in and see my etchings?' but it did the job, and after a quick tour of the house we sat in the lounge, still talking, still eyeing each other up. Horny teenagers on a school trip.

I sat back casually on the sofa, took a deep breath, and turned to face him. Now in my experience there's a point in these situations when you've got to stop the chit-chat and get down to business. A moment when you've got to do nothing except look at the person you're gagging for very late at night, blatantly stare at them until they get the message. It then becomes pretty difficult for the other person to ignore the fact that what you really want to do is stop the mindless conversation and snog.

So I kept looking at Carl. Watching his mouth motoring away. Studying his face. The object of the mission must be to make eye contact, hold it, wait until that precious moment when your head's buzzing because you know the inevitable is just around the corner, seize the opportunity, hold your nerve, lean forward, and swoop in for the kill. Making certain of course that lips are fully locked.

'Tonight's been a laugh, hasn't it?'

'Yeah, it's been good,' I replied, giving him a playful punch on his thigh, and then skilfully resting the flat of my hand on his leg. Good tactic that one. Moment of truth.

Carl looked at my hand.

'Emma said this would happen.'

'What?' I asked, trying not to think about my heart which was thumping so hard by now he must've been able to hear it.

'This.' And that's when he leaned over, met me halfway, and we kissed.

His lips, soft and smooth, touched mine. Hovered for a second, then touched again. He pulled away a fraction, smiled, then drove forward again to kiss me. His stubble brushed my face, and I could feel his breath burning fast and warm on my neck.

Wow.

Music. It fades. Lee undoes a few more buttons on his shirt. It is not completely undone.

LEE

Six months later and my friends were sick to death of hearing about Carl. 'Oh, it's all Carl these days isn't it? Carl, Carl, Carl. You're Carl mad, mun.' They said he was an unhealthy obsession that would end with me in tears on an episode of *Trisha*. But they were only jealous. Like I said - everyone liked Carl. You couldn't help it.

We'd been seeing each other for six-months by now, a sort of anniversary, and Carl wanted to celebrate.

'We should go out.'

'Out?'

'Yeah, well we can't stay in on such a special night. I reckon we should do something.'
'Like what?'
'I don't know. Go to a club or something.'

Club? Club? That'd mean... The 'D' word. Somewhere in the back of my mind I was still having nightmares where I could clearly picture Matthew, jigging up and down to *Come On Eileen* and sharing out a packet of Silk Cut with his friends by the DJ booth. I even wondered whether I'd bump into him. After all, Cardiff city centre on a Saturday night was Matthew's stamping ground. I worried what'd happen if our eyes met across a smoky bar, and planned what I'd say to him just in case sodium did meet water. I chickened out. Let's face it, after my experiences with Matthew, The A-Team had more chance of getting BA Baracus on board a 747 than Carl had of getting me into a club.

'Trust me, I won't make you dance. Honest.'
I looked him in the eye. And believed him.
'Ok. But I'm not going out with you looking like that, you'll have to get changed.'
He was just about to complain when I said, 'Fair's fair, Carl.'
He pulled himself up from the sofa, sighed, and turned to leave the room.
'I'm going to get ready. Five minutes, alright?'

And five minutes later, he was ready.
'Come on. It's Saturday night. We're young, free, and alright, we're not single, but we are living in the fastest growing capital city in Europe.' He always said that. A walking billboard for the Wales Tourist Board. 'Let's go out and make the most of it, yeah?'
I switched off the light and followed him through the door. Another Saturday night in Cardiff.

Sitting in the wine bar on St. Mary's Street we lost track of time and exactly how many units of alcohol our brain cells were absorbing. The place was packed with swaying Cardiffians out for a ball and the live entertainment that was advertised on posters on every available inch of wall.

It was well after I'd started slurring that Lorraine came to the stage and blew hard into her microphone. 'Oh good, it's turned on,' she grinned. 'An' it's not the only thing on this stage tonight that is either!' Lorraine was a vision in denim. Her hair bleached blonde so many times even her roots had forgotten their original colour. Carl returned from the bar with another round and I leapt hungrily at the bag of cheese and onion crisps he was, by now, trained instinctively to get.

'You've been a long time!'

'There was a queue!' And he smiled a wicked smile.

'What? What's going on?'

I was on the verge of finding out.

Lorraine piped up again. 'Now 'en boys an' girls. As you know, Saturday night's entertainment night...' A loud cheer went up. 'Oo, you're a frisky lot tonight, aren't you?' Lorraine thrived for nights like tonight. The centre of attention. 'Well you're not going to be disappointed. Because it's that time of the month again, no, not my time of the month, but the time of the month for karaoke!' And with that word the drunk element of the crowd jumped for joy while the sober element reached for their coats. I was somewhere in the middle. Jumping and reaching. 'An' startin' us off tonight...' The smile on Carl's face was growing. 'A brave young soul...' Getting wider and wider. No way. 'And a cute little thing I'm told too...' I knew what was coming next. 'So give the lad a welcome...' No escape. 'Give a big clap to...' It was too late. 'Lee from Cardiff!'

The crowd barked like wild dogs. Delighted not to be the first victim. 'Come on, Lee. Don't be shy now,' Lorraine ordered. Carl pulled me to my feet, and I had a sudden urge to go dancing, bungee-jumping, swimming in shark infested waters... anything but, anything but, sing!

I'd been set up. Carl, evil boyfriend, had set me up. And as Lorraine dragged me kicking and screaming to the stage, I looked back at Carl and promised revenge.

That stage, right then, was the loneliest place in the world. I was standing there alone, with nothing but a microphone for company, pissed-up, drunk and in possession of a dangerous weapon - my voice. 'Is everyone ready?' I closed my eyes. Reminded myself the ordeal would be over in three minutes. Three minutes and I'd be sitting down again. Three minutes and Carl, who was standing on his chair now, whooping loudly, would be dumped, three minutes... The music kicked in. I realised I didn't even know what song I was supposed to be singing. What had Carl chosen for me? Fuck! What was I meant to...

We hear Tammy Wynetee's 'Stand By Your Man' in karaoke instrumental playing loudly. LEE shuts his eyes as the memory comes flooding home.

Anything but this... Please, anything but...

LEE begins to sing the track. At first, he's dire. Flat, embarrassed, out-of-tune. After the first few lines he pulls away in embarrassment, but then returns to the mike and sings with a little more confidence. Gradually he becomes quite good, until, by the end he's singing brilliantly. The song ends. Applause.

Back at the table, I downed the drink that was waiting for me in one gulp. Carl was laughing raucously and I punched him on the shoulder.
'Oh, come on Shirley Bassey! You must see the funny side?'
Funny, my arse.
'It was a surprise! An anniversary surprise!'
'Surprise? I'd have preferred a surprise like this...'
And it was then that I pulled a small package wrapped in silver paper from my pocket and dropped it onto the table.

'It's not a ring is it? You're not going to ask me to marry you are you?'

'Just open it Carl.'

He undid the paper carefully and lifted up the lid.

'Wow. It's beautiful. Thank you.'

With which he reached over the table and gripped my hand. His new watch shining under the mirror-ball.

We walked up towards the castle in a dream. They'd already hung the Christmas lights and the street was littered with people heading off to clubs. A bunch of students were arguing with a cab driver outside Howells. A man in a bright yellow shirt was chucking up in front of Barclays. We kept walking.

I don't remember crossing the road or what we talked about, but as we approached Sophia Gardens Carl ran on ahead of me. Playing. I ran after him down the path, into the park, and finally caught up with him by one of the tall trees that line the long road up towards the Institute of Sport. He was out of breath, exhilarated. He leaned up against the trunk of a tree.

'I've loved tonight, I've loved the bar, I've loved the entertainment.' He paused to catch his breath. 'I love my watch, and I love....' He hesitated, playing the game we normally played with one another.

'What?' I was supposed to ask. And he would normally reply 'Ewan MacGregor', but tonight he didn't, tonight he was being serious, tonight he said: 'And I love, you.'

It was cold. There were a few clouds in the sky, but not nearly enough to obscure the handful of stars that were still up.

'I do y'know? I love you.'

He kissed me.

'I know,' I told him. I looked him in the eye, and everything was alright.

'Come on wife. Let's go home.'

So hand in hand, we headed for the house.

His hand was the first thing I lost. It's funny because I can still remember exactly what it felt like. Soft, warm, safe. But that night, when we were ripped apart, his hand was the first thing I lost. No more dream. Someone spat, kicked. I remember trying to get up. But scrambling to my feet was useless and I was swept back down to the floor in one move, hard.

'Watch the bender squirm.'
The attackers were laughing and soon there were two men bearing down on me. Punching. Kicking. Grinding their fists into my body. I could hear Carl further along the road shouting, but couldn't make out exactly what he was saying over the jeers of the men. They were shouting so loud, so loud I was sure someone would hear.
'Fancy yourself do you queer? Fancy a bit do you? Go on lads. Give the fucking queer what he fucking deserves.'
I tried to kick. But like the tiny kid getting a hiding on the school yard I was useless. Like the old man attacked in his own front room while he watches TV, I wasn't strong enough. Like the young girl cornered thirty seconds away from her own front door, I couldn't call for help. There were too many. Their punches rained down on top of me. Hail stones on tarmac.
Someone grabbed a fistful of hair and knocked my head against the ground like a drum. Crack. Crack.
A foot struck my stomach, and forced the air from out of me. I wanted to be sick.
The beating stopped. I thought it was over. Innocently prayed they might now let me go. I ached for a second before feeling someone tugging at my clothes. 'No, please, no, don't,' I begged, and looked up again to try and find a human face.
'This'll show the dirty queer. This'll finish it.'

I tried to stop them ripping away my shirt, tried to stop them mauling me, tried to get up and run. Run! The blade pressed into my flesh. 'No, no, don't.' I could feel myself bleeding. Sharp, cold, clean. I knew I was bleeding. 'Please, no.' I looked up again, but all I could see was the shining blade of a Stanley knife coming down for seconds. 'Fuck! No!' Again. Again. The blade tore my skin. Again.

'Get him lower,' someone screamed.

I wriggled, begged them 'No!' But the blade came down again, lower, lower, again lower, and as they slashed at my groin with the knife, I passed out.

Lee undoes the final few buttons on his shirt and shows his scars.

LEE

They've healed. They said all along they would. That they'd get better.

Mum was watching day-time telly when I woke up, chewing on a toffee, and holding my hand. I opened my eyes and watched the TV too for a while, until Mum turned round to unwrap another sweet and saw that I was conscious. She looked at me, tried to say something, but couldn't, and instead, she cried. Dad was just outside. He's never liked hospitals. Always has to leave the room to escape the stench of disinfectant. But he came back in when my mother called. I didn't cry. Not then. I didn't cry until later.

Lee begins to dress.

They stayed all day that day. They were trying to look after me like they had when I was little and home from school with mumps or measles. Dad brought me a pile of magazines. But they weren't the copies of *Smash Hits* and *Look In* he'd fetched home for me when I was still his little boy. He'd chosen more carefully now. *Arena, Sky, What Car?* There was a carrier bag of sweets and fruit. Bottles of Coca-Cola, and a bundle of new clothes, socks, underwear, bought two days earlier from Marks and Spencer and folded neatly inside my bedside locker. They took care of me. They wanted to. But this wasn't chicken pox. And they knew it.

I'd been beaten, kicked, cut, and my parents, had to face me like this, with the bruises and scars on full show, reminding them every time they looked at me what'd happened. And I had to face them. That was the hardest part. I mean, what are you supposed to say to your Mum and Dad when you've been thrashed for being a dirty little queer? When a complete stranger has taken a blade to your balls and cut you, because he didn't like what he saw one night.

It wasn't easy. Embarrassing. Difficult. But not easy. Especially for Mum, who was left to tell me that Carl was also attacked, also beaten, but hadn't been so lucky. How was she meant to explain that he wouldn't be coming through the door with his silly big grin slapped across his face any minute now? Because one Saturday night, one stupid Saturday night, a group of lads got together, had a few cans, and decided to have a laugh.

Dad talked to the police every morning who said they would be pressing for a conviction, but as yet didn't have any definite leads. But they were trying. They told me it was a good thing I hadn't had a chance to go home, shower, change my clothes. There'd be more evidence this way. But why hadn't I stayed to the main road? Why didn't I stay where there were other people who could've seen, could've done something to help? I should've made more noise, I should've got a better view of the attackers, I should've taken a taxi, I should've stayed home, I should've....

I asked Dad to ask them for Carl's watch. I wanted to keep it. Wear it. He came back the next day, and told me they hadn't found a watch. Was it meant to be reported as stolen?

There is only very little light remaining by now.

A week later, when Mum and Dad decided I could probably be left alone for a few hours, I heard a familiar voice in the corridor. A head popped round the door.

'Ooh-lah-lah! Private room? Very swish.'

It was Matthew.

'Now, I've brought you everything you'll need. Moisturiser: vitally important because we don't want to go sacrificing our good looks now do we? After all, you never know which way these doctors are inclined. Some tapes of that terrible noise you like listening to, Travis I ask you, and a box of Ferrero Rocher. But don't go eating them all at once otherwise you'll put on even more weight, and I don't want to be held responsible for that.'

He danced around the room, joking and laughing before finally crash landing on the edge of my bed.

'Ooh. Quite comfy isn't it?'

He smiled.

'Well? How's the patient?'

And that's when I cried.

So, Matthew hugged me, and stayed until I stopped.

Silence. Blackout.

Frank Vickery has been writing plays for more than thirty years. His first play, *After I'm Gone*, was produced in 1978 and won The Howard De Waldon trophy for the best one-act play in the UK. He then went on to create and write prolifically for The Parc and Dare Theatre Company, before branching out to write scores of TV and radio scripts. He celebrated his twenty-fifth stage play last year. All of his plays are published by Samuel French Ltd, London.

For the last ten years he has been writing for The Sherman Theatre, Cardiff, and now runs his own theatre company, Grassroots Productions.

Sleeping With Mickey

Frank Vickery

This play was first produced in July, 1992 at the Sherman
Theatre, Cardiff.

Eileen - **Menna Trussler**
Director - **Phil Clarke**

A sort of bed-sit. The living area has a small cottage-type two-seater sofa and a small table with a tray, glass and bottle of sherry on it. A Christmas tree stands rather forlornly in a corner and a television set and a long low coffee table take up just about all of the remaining space. Behind the living area is the bedroom. There is a single bed with the blankets turned neatly back; a table beside the bed has a small reading lamp on it. The curtains are drawn closed at the back, where there is a window (never seen) that looks out onto the street.
It's New Year's Eve. Christmas has come and gone, and the ambience of the room should echo this.

When the lights come up, Eileen is sitting on the sofa watching the television. She has a copy of the TV Times open on her lap and the handset of the television in her hand. She is checking programmes from the magazine against the ones she is putting up on the screen.

EILEEN

Pathetic, isn't it? New Year's Eve, and here I am stuck in front of my twenty five inch NICAM stereo with remote control, four hundred and thirty nine pounds, and what's my choice?

Reading from the magazine

Down and Out in Beverly Hills, I can't bloody stand Bette Midler...

Turning over with the remote

This is Spinal Tap, an hilarious spoof rockumentary...

She stares at the screen for a brief moment

Nothing to keep me conscious there.

Turning over again

Clive James. A wry and dry look back over the year's events. God, I think I'd rather contemplate suicide.

Not happy with anything she has found, she resorts to switching the television off.
She stands.

I mean I'm not asking for much. I've got my little bottle of sherry here.

She indicates

All I want to go with it is a nice film.

Moving behind the sofa

Oh what I wouldn't give to watch Ronald Coleman and Greer Garson in Random Harvest. I seen it six times. I've seen Star Wars five and I don't even like it.

A slight pause

It's not on when you think about it, is it? It's not the pound for the magazine I begrudge, no... it's the ninety-five pounds a year for the licence that allows me to see the new year in with Clive James, that's nothing short of day light robbery.

Pause

I could have gone out. I didn't have to be stuck here. The couple across the road are having a bit of a fling, if that's the right word for it, and they asked me round. They're not my type. Nice enough but they're vegetarians... you know the sort. Thonged sandals and no socks... even in this weather. She makes all her own Christmas cards and he's very keen on needle-point. He's very good at it too, I've seen some of his pieces. 'Come over and have a drink and something to eat with us,' he said. No thank you, I thought. You can imagine what they're having, can't you? Soya chicken vol-au-vents and open sandwiches of cold broccoli and nuts. Well that's what they forced on me the last time I went over there and I only popped across to ask if they had change of fifty pee.

A slight pause

Have you ever tasted cold broccoli? I nearly threw up all over their rush mats.

A slight pause

I've half a mind to go to bed but I won't sleep, I know I won't.

She looks at her watch

Twenty past eleven. What am I going to do for the next forty minutes?

She looks around the room

I could take down the Christmas tree and put the cards away. I usually do it on the first of January anyway, I can't stick them any longer than that.

Another slight pause

Or I could go to town on the sherry...

Making up her mind

No, I know what I'll do... I'll wrap a Christmas present. Now I know what you're thinking. You're thinking I'm off my head, aren't you? Well I'm not.

She gathers together a piece of Christmas wrapping paper, sellotape and a box which contains the gift.

I do this every year. Well Christmas isn't any fun otherwise. You see there's only me now and whatever gifts I have, I have to buy myself... but I don't like knowing what I'm having. As you can appreciate, you can't buy something a few weeks before and be pleasantly surprised when you open it on Christmas morning. What I do is buy something at this time of year, wrap it up and put it away in the back of a cupboard. I had this beautiful cardigan from myself this year and I didn't know a thing about it.

A slight pause

I had a real bargain this year in the Boxing Day sales.

She holds up the box

It's a very delicate vase. I won't show it to you. I haven't seen it since I left the shop and the sooner I forget about it the better. I think it's got freesias spilling down the front. They're my favourite flower. That's what I had in my bouquet when I got married.

A slight pause

I thought a vase would be nice... well you never know when I might want to send myself flowers.

She continues to wrap the box

This is pretty paper, isn't it? Ten sheets for a pound. I'll buy a few more things in the next month or two. I've known me have as many as eight or nine presents to open on a Christmas morning. You've got to make the effort, haven't you? It's just another day otherwise.

A slight pause

I read in one of my magazines that some people who live alone, and women as much as men apparently, just let the day pass without as much as a sprig of holly on the mantlepiece. I don't believe in that. It's only once a year and if you don't put anything in to it you can't get anything out, that's what I say. I don't hold back on anything, me. I even buy a box of crackers... even though I don't have anyone to pull them with... it doesn't bother me, I pull them with myself.

She laughs a little

Mind you, I did burn my chin one year. Nothing serious, I frightened myself more than anything.

She finishes wrapping the vase

Now I wonder if this will go under the bed.

She tries and it does

Oh yes, there you are.

She puts the Christmas paper and sellotape away

Well that's one done.

A slight pause

Now what else?

She briefly glances around the room

Do you know, if I'm not sitting down in front of the television I've got to be doing something.

She decides to collect up all the Christmas cards. She stops and smiles as she looks at one in particular.

Remember me saying they make their own Christmas cards across the way? Well this is the one I had from them. It's made out of wall-paper... and the envelope it came in. It's easy enough to do, I watched that little girl do it on Blue Peter. I wouldn't send out cards like it myself, but still, it's the thought that counts.

She opens it and reads aloud

To Eileen. Merry Christmas and a Happy New Year. From Fabian and Lorraine. You know, any other names just wouldn't be right for that pair.

She collects up the remaining cards

I did say I wasn't going to send any cards this year, but I was here one evening looking for a screwdriver, the fuse had gone on my facial toner I had for Christmas the year before last, and I found a box of cards I'd completely forgotten about. It seemed a pity not to use them. I like to see a few around the room anyway, and if I don't send any I don't get any, it's as simple as that. Oh I know I didn't have to put a stamp on them and post them, but if I hadn't I was afraid the postman would have realised the only mail he delivered here over Christmas was bills. Anyway, I'm not harming anyone... and it does help the place look that little more festive.

She opens and reads, with pleasure, another card

To Eileen. Have a lovely Christmas and hope you have some company in the New Year. Love and best wishes, Eileen. I don't know why I wrote that. I'm quite happy on my own.

Insisting

No, really I am.

She looks at the cards in her hand before she tosses them to the floor. A slight pause as she comes to sit down on the sofa.

I didn't know how I was going to cope when I lost Linda, but I'm all right and she's been gone six years now.

Doing a quick mental check

Yes that's right, it's six years but it's the seventh Christmas.

A slight pause

I always knew I would have her for ever but I kept her until she was twenty-eight so I can't complain.

A slight pause

I do miss her though... what mother wouldn't.

A slight pause

When they said I had a baby girl they didn't tell me there was anything wrong. I didn't know a thing until the following day. Doctor King came to see me, he was my gynaecologist. He sat at the bottom of the bed and started talking about chromosomes. We've all got forty-six and apparently little Linda had forty-seven.

A slight pause as she reflects

Who would think that one little chromosome would make all that difference... but it did... and not only to Linda but to me too because it changed my life.

Getting up

We were both confused and hurt at the time. I say, 'we', I mean Ted and me. Ted was Linda's father.

Reaching for a photograph which she shows to the audience

Here he is on the day we got married.

A slight pause

I don't know where he is now. Couldn't even get in touch with him when Linda died. He probably wouldn't have turned up even if he knew.

A slight pause

He couldn't cope, you see. There are a lot of people like that.

A slight pause

I did hear a rumour about a year ago that he was living with a woman in Pinner and had three perfect children.

She replaces the photo frame

Me and Linda were all right though. Oh it was hard in the beginning, but as soon as she able to go to school I went back to work. Ted left before her second birthday.

We thought everything was going to be wonderful when I fell pregnant.

Moving left of the sofa

The day I told Ted he went out and bought this fabulous Swan pram. It was huge... could hardly get it through into the hall. Any bigger and I think we might have to have had it taxed and insured. I remember it cost twenty-four pounds nineteen and eleven. We kept it covered in the front room not for the dust to get at it for practically the whole of the nine months. It was Ted's pride and joy.

Linda was mine.

Funny how life has a way of dealing you a card from the bottom of the deck though, isn't it? Well, that's the way Ted looked at it anyway.

A slight pause

Linda was born on the fourth of July, American Independence Day. Mothers tended to rest up for a good couple of weeks in those days so it must have been about the end of July or even the beginning of August before we took her out in the pram for the first time. It was a Saturday I remember and a beautiful day, really hot. Lots of little boys wore laced canvas shoes, shorts and printed tee-shirts. Sloppy-joes they were called then. It was nineteen fifty four.

It took ages before we actually stepped out wheeling this magnificent four-wheel work of art. I'd been ready for a time, it was Ted who was dragging his feet. I should have realised then there was something bothering him but all my attention was on Linda. He had suggested a couple of times that I take her out on my own... or maybe I should start without him and he'd catch up later, but I wasn't having any of it. I wanted us both to walk down that street pushing our baby and be as proud as the next couple. What I didn't realise of course was that was exactly what Ted was dreading.

A slight pause

You see, we hadn't talked about... well about the fact that Linda was a little 'Downs' baby. I tried bringing it up a few times but he made it obvious he wasn't ready. He never was ready as it turned out... which was why in the end he felt he couldn't stay with us.

The biggest shame of all of course was he never saw her grow up, or knew her as a person. You see when we did eventually talk he had this preconceived idea, like a lot of people, of what Downs are like... it turned out that Linda wasn't typical, but he didn't stay around long enough to find out.

A slight pause

She was termed 'high grade', which meant she was much more advanced than most. Oh she'd never pass the eleven plus or drive a car or anything, but she did work at Remploy for ten years.

Smiling proudly

She could even play the piano. Nothing difficult but she could read more music than I could. She knew enough for us to get through a couple of carols at Christmas. That was when I had a piano of course, and before I came to live in this place.

A slight pause

Anyway, there we were, the three of us, me, Ted and baby Linda off out for the morning. Ted, as I said, was a bit reluctant, but I was ready and more than willing to show off our little addition.

A slight pause

Word had got out of course that we'd had a little 'Downs' baby and generally people were very good. They either crossed the road and pretended not to see us, or they stopped to have a short chat and lied.

I didn't blame the ones who ignored us. I understood perhaps they didn't want to and probably panicked because they didn't know what to say. Then there were the others. The ones who couldn't resist having a little peep. There was one woman I remember who stopped and asked how I was, and before I had chance to answer she'd stuck her head under the canopy to have a look at Linda. Oh, she said... she looks quite normal. Then looked me straight in the eye and said, 'Mind you, she is sleeping'.

A slight pause

Some people told us how pretty she was and meant it... some said it and didn't. Others couldn't say anything at all and just squeezed my arm as if in commiseration, you know, like as if there'd been a death in the family. Everybody deals with it in their own way I suppose.

Ted said he couldn't understand how I wasn't upset by it all. He didn't just mean about our first day out, he was talking about Linda's medical condition and everything it meant. But you see... after the initial disappointment I accepted the fact we had a little 'Downs' for a daughter and felt all that was left to do was get on with our lives.

Sitting on the sofa

When she was a couple of months old we nearly lost her. Lots of Downs have respiratory problems and Linda was asthmatic. She was critical for days and we were told it could go either way. I'm not a religious person but I do believe in God, and the only time I left her bed was to go and pray. After she was out of the woods and back home with us I told Ted I'd been praying for her and do you know what he said to me? Now Ted is someone who doesn't believe in anything. He said he'd been praying for her too. The only difference was, I was praying for her to live.

A slight pause

They say everything has a reason and I honestly believe Linda had to be ill at that time in order for me to find out exactly how Ted was feeling. We both knew he had no place with us after that and it wasn't long before he left.

He didn't take anything with him. It was an ordinary day just like any other and I didn't suspect a thing. He left for work then rang about lunch time to say he wouldn't be home for tea because he had to get away for a few days. He said he'd arranged some time off and would ring me from where ever it was he would find himself. He knew he wouldn't be coming back... and so did I.

A slight pause before she gets up from the sofa

Oh he kept in touch over the telephone, and he was very good financially... I can't say he dodged his responsibilities in that department. He supported Linda right up until the day she started work. But do you know, in the seventeen years he'd left us and God knows how many telephone calls and letters, he never once mentioned her. No birthday card, Christmas present, nothing. A nice cheque for me which I knew by the amount included something for Linda, but in lots of ways he wanted to wipe her out ... pretend she didn't happen. I never used to let him get off the hook that easily, though. I was always talking about her. I mean I understood his reaction to a point, but the older she became the more proud I was, and the more proud I was the more embarrassed he seemed to be. I never understood that.

A slight pause

When she was about eight I asked her what she wanted for Christmas and she said, 'A Daddy'. I told her he was dead so she asked for a Post Office set instead.

A slight pause

I did meet someone after Ted left. Linda must have been about six... well she was in school anyway because that's where I met him. John.

The headmistress Miss Prothoroe took six months off for ill health... she had a hysterectomy with complications or something and John was posted in to take over. He was from a place called Ashton which is just outside Manchester. I got to know everything about him and I'd only met him twice.

Nothing went on in that school that the 'Mothers' didn't discuss outside the school gate.

A slight pause

Anyway, the post was filled so quickly he didn't have time to arrange proper accommodation. Someone said he was staying in some bed and breakfast place until he had time to sort things out. Well I felt a bit awkward, you know. I mean there was only me and Linda living in a three bedroom house... it seemed selfish not to offer help even if he refused. Well needless to say he didn't, he jumped at the offer. Oh, it was all above board. He had his own room and everything, there was never any funny business... but the rest of the mothers had a field day as you can imagine.

A slight pause

He was marvellous with Linda and she thought the world of him. He was just like a father to her... mind you, he was nothing like a husband to me. Now that was all right until one day it bothered me. And the day I knew it bothered me was the day I knew I was in love with him... and I can pin point the moment. The three of us were at the table having tea together and Linda sneezed. Before I had chance, or Linda come to that, he'd taken a handkerchief from his pocket, wiped her nose, cleaned her glasses and blessed... all without a minute's hesitation. He didn't even look up. I'm glad he didn't though because if he had he'd have seen my face and he'd have known exactly how I felt about him.

She has a thought

Nothing could ever come of it... well that's what I kept telling myself. It was never any secret he had a wife back home. He never talked about her much and I rarely asked any questions in that direction, but I did hear from one of the other mothers, but this was before he moved in - they stopped telling me things after that - that she had a sick mother that lived with them so there was never any question of her ever coming down to visit him... and do you know, in all the time he lived with us he never once went and visited them. It was a very strange set-up. He must have loved her though because the minute Miss Prothoroe returned to work, John returned to Ashton.

A slight pause

Linda broke her heart and showed it... for me it wasn't that easy... but like everything else life throws at us, I just picked myself up, dusted myself down, but didn't as the song says, 'Start all over again'.

Oh, I wanted to. I had the odd drink, you know... one or two meals out but nothing that led to anything. And sex was never that important to me... well, not, that is, until I met Carlton.

When I said sex wasn't important, I didn't mean I didn't enjoy it...

far from it, but... when Linda came along, especially in the beginning, she was very demanding. I didn't have time to eat properly in those days let alone anything else. No, when Ted left that was the last thing I missed.

A slight pause

I did want to sleep with John from Ashton, though. I used to lay awake in bed at night waiting for the door to open. One time it did and I thought my heart was going to jump out of my chest... but it was only Linda wanting a glass of water.

A slight pause

He was such a gentleman... I used to wonder years later if he used to lie in his bed and wait for me in the same way. Wouldn't it have been sad if he had? Wouldn't it have been just my luck?

That's something I haven't enjoyed very much of, you know... luck. Linda aside, you could never say I've been a lucky person. Not that I consider myself unlucky... no, it's just... well, what can I tell you.

She thinks of something

Yes. My father gave me a hundred premium bonds for my fortieth birthday. I'm fifty...

She waves her hand, not wanting to be specific.

... now and I've never won a brass farthing. Idwal -

Pointing to the ceiling

- bought six last year and has won two fifty pounds already. Incredible, isn't it?

I haven't told you about Idwal, have I? He's got one of the flats upstairs. Plenty of money. Anyway, I'd only been living here about a fortnight when I bumped into him in the hall. I was taking in my milk and he'd just taken his dog for a walk. I started to suspect something wasn't quite right when he spent fifteen minutes the following week telling me about his horse. I don't know to this day what made me ask him where he kept it but the minute he said the bathroom I know what I was dealing with. I had a marvellous conversation with him yesterday about the mating habits of the Wildebeest. He's a refreshing change from the veggies across the way I can tell you. He's got a social worker apparently, but then so have I. The only difference is he introduces her to everyone as his mother.

A slight pause

Anyway, as I was saying, he may be halfway round the twist but he's born lucky. I remember when we all bought tickets for the Christmas hamper... when I say all I mean everyone in the block. I bought so many I'd have been better off making up a hamper myself. Idwal bought one. I don't have to tell you who got first prize... and he's always the same.

I sound jealous don't I, but I'm not. Well a teensy weensy bit envious perhaps.

He won a trip for two to Disney World back in the summer and he wasn't going to go. You're off your head, I said. Then quickly re-phrased as soon as I realised what I'd said.

He didn't go anyway in the end because rumour had it he swapped the tickets with someone on the fourth floor for two guinea-pigs, a copy of the Sunday Times and a ferret.

A slight pause

Disney World really is a marvellous place... I've been there. I had a wonderful time there and I didn't think I was going to go.

You see the trip didn't come about anything like as planned. It all started a good couple of years before Linda died. I don't know why, but I had this thing about taking her there. Linda was never keen on the idea which surprised me because even though she was twenty-eight at the time she always enjoyed the cartoons.

A slight pause

Anyway, I promised myself I'd try and save to get the money to go. Well... weeks turned in months and I wasn't getting off to a very good start. The minute I managed to put something away I'd have an unexpected bill, or Linda would need something. Although she was working she wasn't really earning enough to keep herself. I'd more or less shelved the idea when I had a letter from a solicitor in Cardiff telling me that my father had died.
Now, he had re-married about a year before Linda was born. She seemed very nice and was about fifteen years younger than him – not that there was anything wrong in that.

A slight pause

She didn't want to live in the house which was still very much full of my mother - understandable - so they sold up and went to live in Splott. Now why anyone would want to live in Splott is beyond me, but there you are, it was their choice and anyway they seemed to be happy there... or so I thought. It wasn't until my father had died that I came to know they hadn't been together for the past eight months. She was living with a half-caste in Grangetown. They hadn't actually divorced but he did leave a will bequeathing everything to me. Needless to say she contested it and the whole thing got messy resulting in a very long wait before I had access to his estate.

I sold the house in Splott... well wouldn't you? And so suddenly the Disney trip was back on.

I tried to book it so that we'd be out there for Linda's birthday - I guessed there'd be some sort of celebration it being Independence Day, and it would all add to making the trip that little bit extra special... but that old thing called 'luck' popped its ugly little head up again and we couldn't book in. The earliest date we could get was September the tenth.

A slight pause

It's a strange old world though, isn't it - because on July the fifth Linda went to sleep and never woke up. She came home from work as she usually did and dozed off on the settee, but always came round in time for 'Neighbours'.

A slight pause

It was bad enough happening here, imagine what it would have been like if we'd been in America.

A slight pause

My world came to an end for a while. It took a long time for me to learn to cope. I can't say you get over it because I don't think a parent ever gets over the death of a child.

A slight pause

Well... here I was, eight months on just having gone through my first Christmas and New Year on my own. Depressed wasn't the word.

The last eight months had dragged by because I hadn't done

anything with them. I wasn't keeping house, keeping warm, nothing. I was letting everything go. I was letting myself go. I'd lost about three stone in weight because I wasn't eating properly - with the result that when I did decide to put on a different frock it was swimming on me. Nothing in my wardrobe was any good.

A slight pause

I couldn't cry anymore... I don't think I had a tear left in my body. Then, at my lowest ebb I think I must have had a brainstorm because I started emptying almost everything out of my wardrobe. I went into Linda's room for the first time and started doing in the same in there.

The minute I walked into her room I suppose I took the first step towards getting myself back together. I knew it was a big thing for me to do because I'd avoided doing it for all those months, and now, here I was, standing outside the door gripping the handle and waiting for the courage to turn it. When I did, the first thing I saw was this mass of colour on the window-sill. Linda had a Christmas cactus and it was in full flower. How it was still alive was beyond me. I know they don't need a lot of water but it was the middle of summer when I was in there last.

A slight pause

Anyway, it was very nice to see it in bloom. I took it as a sign. It was time to start putting things back together.

It took me about a fortnight to get the house looking the way it used to, and when that was done I started on myself. I did what I could with my hair, put on what glad-rags I had left from the clear-out and sampled my first taste of fresh air for what felt like the best part of a year. I felt better than I had in a long time. I didn't know where I was going, I just followed my feet. I was passing the train station and the next thing I knew I could hear myself asking for a return ticket to Cardiff Central. I had a field day. After having my hair done I bought myself a whole new wardrobe. I don't know how I carried it all home.

Walking back from the station I passed a travel agent's. I stopped, and again I don't know why. Smack right in front of me at eye level was one of those cards - you know the sort. It said, 'Orlando. Fourteen nights. Fly Gatwick. Four hundred and ninety-nine pounds'. I went the first week in May. Nervous wasn't the word... but I needn't have been. They were marvellous to me. From the time I set foot on the plane, and I'd never flown before, to the time I came back. Well that's how much I enjoyed myself, I didn't want to come back... and I very nearly didn't !

A slight pause

Accommodation out there is wonderful compared to this country. I stayed at the Continental Plaza on International Drive. When they showed me to my room I couldn't believe it. The first thing I noticed was there were two double beds in it. Two. Oh my God, I thought, I'm sharing... but I wasn't. It was all for little old me.

I didn't do or see anything much when I got there. All I wanted to do was to climb into one of those beds and catch up on some sleep which I did. When I woke up I didn't know if it was eight o'clock in the morning or eight o'clock in the night. It wasn't until after I'd had my bath that I managed to work it out. It's not late, I thought, and I'd never sleep right through now... so I put something nice on and had a walk round the hotel. They had this huge lounge and I ended up having a drink in there. I ended up having a drink in there most nights as it turned out, because that's where I met him... Carlton. I'd only just sat down at the table when there he was. He looked very smart in his waiter's uniform. You can say what you like, these Americans really do know how to look after you. Every time I emptied my glass he was there ready with a refill. It was never anyone else... always him. Carlton, I said, what if I didn't want another one, I meant a drink. What if I wanted to have something different? Then he paused and looked me straight in the eye... and that's when it happened. I wasn't sure what at the time but it didn't take me long to work out.

A slight pause as she gets up from the sofa and pours another drink

I must have been on my sixth or seventh gin when I sensed someone coming to sit next to me.

Sitting back on the sofa

When I looked up it was him. I didn't notice at first but he had two drinks with him this time... and there was something else different about him as well but for a second I didn't know what it was... then I realised, he was out of his uniform. He had finished his shift and had come to join me for a drink. These people are so polite you couldn't say no to them even if you wanted to... not that I wanted to of course. Here I was in a foreign country and in a strange hotel I was grateful for any kind of company.

A slight pause

We sat and had a couple more drinks and he told me his life story. I don't know if all he said was true because I don't think I was listening. All I was aware of was I couldn't take my eyes off his face... his eyes in particular. I've never in my life seen eyes that colour before. The only way I can describe them is... Mediterranean blue... or green... or something in between. You know, you often see it in that holiday programme with Judith Chalmers. It's a sort of turquoise...

She says it again, pronouncing it differently

Turquoise. He had black eyebrows with a moustache to match. His nose was... perfect, and his lips gave me regular glimpses of the whitest teeth I'd ever seen. His hair was immaculate, not a strand out of place. Mine was a mess in comparison, but I'd had too many drinks by this time to question his attention.

A slight pause

Eventually, I don't know how much later, I stood up.

She stands up

I must have swayed a little because he suggested we go for a walk. He was twenty-six and I was knocking forty...

She waves her hand not wishing to be specific

... who was I to refuse.

A slight pause

We didn't go very far... just around the hotel. Then he showed me to my room. We were walking down the corridor towards it. 'Oh my God, I thought. He wants to come in.' Half of me was afraid he was going to suggest it and the other half was afraid he wasn't. He asked me for my key and I rummaged in my bag and gave it to him. He opened the door and I walked in. When I turned round he was still standing on the outside holding my keys towards me. I walked back over to him and he dropped them into the palm of my hand. Then he smiled, said goodnight and left.

I had a good night's sleep and thought, 'Well, that was the end of that...' but the following day I found myself looking for him. I couldn't see him anywhere in the hotel and I didn't have the courage to ask for him by name.

A slight pause

I went and spent the day at Sea World. Linda would have loved it. I was gone all day and had lunch and supper out. I didn't get back to my room till gone nine so it must have been about tenish by the time I walked into the hotel bar. I didn't have the chance to see if I could see him, before I could draw breath he was there beside me showing me to a table.

She laughs and smiles as she remembers

And that's what it was like for most of the time I was there. He'd finish his shift, stay and have a drink with me, see me to my room and then go. He never once asked to come in and I never offered.

I saw him every night but never in the day. Every time I asked him about that he either didn't answer me or he'd change the subject. He did tell me that working in the hotel wasn't his main employment, but I couldn't get him to talk about what else he did. I gave up asking in the second week. I knew if I kept bringing it up I might upset him in some way and he might not spend as much time with me and I didn't want that to happen.

A slight pause

It was the last night before I flew home. I got out of the lift and stepped out into the hotel lobby. What shall I do, I thought. Do I go into the restaurant and have my evening meal now? Or shall I go into the lounge and have an aperitif? I'll have an aperitif.

Much to my disappointment he didn't meet me at the door. I looked around but couldn't see him. Another waiter offered to show me to a table but I quickly decided I didn't want to stay. Just as I was turning to leave I spotted him sitting at the bar. He was wearing his own clothes which meant he was off duty. I sat next to him and we had two or three drinks together. Everything was all right except I was beginning to get a little depressed because I knew it was our last time together.

All of a sudden he finished his drink, stood up and apologised. Oh... you're not going, I said? He explained he had something to do that couldn't be put off. Suddenly I stood up as well. Oh, I said... you're not going to leave a lady on her own... on her birthday... are you?

A slight pause

He smiled the broadest smile, then gave me a row for not telling him before. He ordered more drinks and we sat at a table this time.

I don't know how many, but several drinks later he asked if I'd eaten. When I said I hadn't we moved into the restaurant and spent the rest of the evening there. I'd been there two weeks but this was the first time we'd eaten together. I told him everything about me that night. I told him things I hadn't shared with anyone. It had taken a fortnight, but here I was taking off all my clothes, metaphorically speaking of course, and having dinner in a restaurant sitting opposite this beautiful young man which I knew by now I wanted more than anything.

Before I knew it we were stepping out of the lift and walking the maze of corridors that led to my room. The time it took should have seemed longer because neither of us were making any conversation, but it didn't, instead we seemed to have got to my door in record time. He opened it as he always did and handed me my key. 'What time is your flight tomorrow?' he said. I told him the taxi wasn't picking me up until quarter past two. 'I won't be able to see you off,' he said. 'I start work at ten and won't be through till five.'

A slight pause

So... this is it, I thought. 'Better say goodbye now then, is it?' I said. He gave me a lovely look. I thanked him for his company and kissed him on his neck. He didn't flinch. He swallowed, and the only time I took my eyes off his was to look at his Adam's apple as it moved slowly up and down. I didn't look up again until he was walking down the corridor. I'm forty...

Again she doesn't admit her age

... I thought, what could he possibly see in me.

A slight pause

My God he looked lovely even from behind.

A slight pause

I watched him go, and just as he was about to disappear he put his hand up on the wall. Oh, I thought, he's going to give me some sort of wave... but he wasn't... he was only hugging the corner as he turned it. All I could see now was his hand and the cuff of his shirt.

Calling:

Carlton ! I shouted... and he stopped. His hand stayed there for a minute... then disappeared. I couldn't believe it. He did hear me, I know he did. I was just about to run after him when all of a sudden there he was... he had turned back and was walking towards me. Panic set in. Oh my God, I thought, what am I going to say to him... but I needn't have worried. I didn't have to say a word. In fact, neither of us said anything until it was all over and we were laying back on the bed together.

It wasn't dirty... or rough. In fact it was just the opposite. He was so gentle. I'd never experienced anything like it before or since. Sex with Ted all those years ago was fine but nothing compared to this. For the first time in my life I felt I'd been made love to and I wanted to do it again... so we did. This time I made love to him.

The third time we did it we did it for each other. After that we ran out of reasons but we did it all the same. I couldn't believe where all this energy was coming from.

A slight pause

We did talk a lot in between and eventually he told me he worked in the day at Disney World.

I've got a confession to make, he said. Oh God, I thought, what the hell is he going to tell me now. Earlier on down in the bar...I didn't have to rush off. I lied. Oh that's alright, I said. I lied too. He said, you did? I said, yes... it's not my birthday.

We did eventually go to sleep. When I woke up I was in bed by myself. My God I thought, I dreamt it. I knew I'd had a good couple of drinks, but did I really dream it? I went and had a bath and all the time I kept trying to work it out. It all seemed real enough... it must have happened. Then the more I thought about it the more convinced I was it couldn't have.

A slight pause

I remember drying my hair and thinking... well, whether it happened or not it was wonderful anyway. I talked myself into hoping it was a dream. I knew if it had happened there was no possibility of it ever happening again, but if it was a dream? Well who knows, it might be one of those recurring ones.

A slight pause

The thing is... I've never been able to get him out of my mine... never. Even now he's still part of my life.

Pause

I was all packed and ready to go but had a couple of hours to spare
before I was due to leave for the airport. I remembered him telling
me he worked at Disney World in the day but that could have
been all part of the dream for all I knew. I had nothing better to
do so I got in a taxi and went there. I knew in my heart I wouldn't
see him but that didn't stop me looking. I must have been there
about an hour when the midday parade started. That's when all
the Disney characters do a walk about. There was a party of
children that must have come from some sort of special school.
The type Linda would have gone to had she been born about
twenty years later. There's lots of them now but they didn't exist
in Linda's day. Anyway, there must have been about twenty or
thirty children there in all. They were having a great time having
their photographs taken with Snow White. The dwarfs were there
too of course and so was Goofy, Minnie and Mickey. I just stood
there looking on wondering what Linda would have made of it all.

A slight pause

It was time for the Disney lot to move on and they all turned to
leave... except Mickey, who was looking over in my direction. He
waved. He can't be waving at me, I thought, but there was no-one
else there. So I waved back, and as I did I had the strangest
feeling... it couldn't be... could it? I started to walk towards him.
As I got nearer he turned to look how far the others had gone.
They were dancing for another group of kids about fifty yards
away. I was so near him now, I could almost touch him. I stopped
and tried to see where they look out from. Then I spotted it. I
could barely make out a face behind a piece of black net which
must have only been about three inches square. He didn't give me
a chance to have another look, before I knew it he turned and ran
to join the others. I watch him until they all moved on again. He
was the last to go. He didn't look back. They all walked on and he

disappeared with the rest, but as he did he put his hand up on the wall hugging the corner as he went. The last thing I saw was Mickey's white glove and the cuff of blue tailed coat. Carlton, I shouted.

The Disney recording of 'When You Wish Upon A Star' begins, quite loudly at first with the harps etc, then playing beneath Eileen's words.

And he stopped. His hand stayed there for a minute... then disappeared. I waited... nothing. This time I knew he wasn't going to turn back.

Blackout as the vocals begin on 'When You Wish Upon A Star'.

ACT TWO

A few minutes have passed. The television is on and the volume is quite loud. Thousands of people are celebrating at Trafalgar Square. The chimes of Big Ben can be clearly heard as the lights come up in the living room.
Eileen is standing in front of the television. She is holding up a glass of sherry and singing.

EILEEN

For auld lang syne my dear, for auld lang syne, we'll drink a cup of kindness yet for the sake of auld lang syne.

She drinks her sherry in one and then immediately switches off the television with the handset

It's all right to watch on television, but who the hell wants to be at Trafalgar Square at this time of night...
I don't that's for sure.

She tosses the handset on the sofa as she turns and pours herself another drink

Well... that's another year wrapped up and tucked away.

Having poured the sherry, she leaves it for a moment on the small table and comes to sit down on the sofa. She takes one of the small cushions and hugs it to her tummy.

A slight pause

It's a funny old time, isn't it? Now I mean, after the bells. A lot of people find it exciting not knowing what's to come, a clean sheet so to speak. I'd give anything to have one of those, let me tell you. I know exactly what's in store for me. Others think it's a terribly sad time. They're the ones who are hanging on to something they'd rather not let go of. I've never known what to make of it myself, New Year's Eve.

A slight pause

It's impossible not to think of Linda of course. Not that we ever saw the new year in together, she could never keep awake. I always crept in and gave her a kiss before I went to bed though... I miss that.

I haven't kissed anyone since...

A smile grows and spreads across her face as she remembers

I wonder where he is now... my little Mickey Mouse?

Quite excited at the thought

Oh there's nothing I wouldn't give to have him knock on my door now this minute and wish me a Happy New Year. He's not going to of course, but that still doesn't stop me thinking about it. I gave him my address, you see. Not this one, I hadn't moved to this place then... and because of that it's given me the licence to dream... and of course, you don't have to be asleep to do it. One of the reasons I didn't want to move here was the thought that he wouldn't be able to find me should he ever try and look... but then I thought, one move wouldn't stop him finding me.

A slight pause

I've more or less given up on the idea now, but there's still a part of me that thinks maybe one day he'll turn up at my door.

This pleasant thought leaves her as she gets up and wanders around the back of the sofa. Her face has a different expression now.

I didn't adapt very well to coming home from America. How I got on the plane in Orlando I'll never know. I didn't realise it at the time but I was going into some sort of depression again. I didn't unpack for a week... I just couldn't face it. Then when I did, the first thing I came across was my camera. When I took it out I had four shots left which meant I had thirty-two of Carlton. I did manage to get into a couple of them... He asked a waiter friend to take one of us sitting at a table one night, and I asked a little old lady to take one of us standing together under a cherry tree which was in full bloom at the back of the hotel. I showed her what button to press and in all fairness she did exactly what I'd asked. We were standing very close to each other and he slipped his arm around my waist. He was giving one of his famous smiles and it would have been a perfect picture if nature hadn't stepped in and spoiled it.

A slight pause

When I had the courage to take the film to be developed, that particular photograph was ruined because of a little white petal that fell from the tree and happened to be level with the end of his lip when the shot was taken. It distorted the whole feature of his mouth and made him look grotesque. He looked as if he had a huge fang growing out of the end if it. I tore it up and threw it in the bin... even though it was quite a nice one of me.

Anyway, the other photographs turned out all right and they were all I had left to hang on to for a while... well, for about three or four months, anyway.

I hadn't been feeling up to the mark and made an appointment to see my doctor. He referred me to a specialist who told me the problem immediately. Rubbish, I said. I want a second opinion... but I didn't need one. He showed me the screen of the sound scan machine and I could see the little heart beat for myself. I was confused and more than a little disorientated. Here I was at forty-something... pregnant by someone I had totally convinced myself up to then I'd only dreamt I'd slept with.

A slight pause before she smiles

It didn't take me long to get used to the idea of having his baby though. I didn't care what people thought... I've never cared about things like that. I was feeling very pleased with myself, and why shouldn't I? I had proof positive now that it really happened between us and I was more than thrilled to be having something that was going to physically bind us together for the rest of my life... something permanent to hang on to... or so I thought.

A slight pause

Nothing ever goes the way you expect it to though, does it?

A slight pause

I had a little man come in to turn the small bedroom into a nursery, oh I was well into the swing of it by this time. It was about time for elevenses and I'd just taken him up a tray of tea and biscuits when there was a knock at the front door. 'Excuse me,' I said. 'Help yourself to sugar and milk.'

I had a glass front door in those days, well to the half anyway, and although it was patterned I was always able to make out certain people if they were already known to me. You know, the milkman, the baker, that sort of thing.

I could tell from the outline it was a man. I checked my hair in the hall mirror and he knocked again before I had chance to answer. When I did I was taken aback. It was my doctor. 'Oh, I think there's some mistake,' I said. 'I haven't put in a call.' He said he knew that but he wanted to have a chat with me. He followed me into the lounge and the two of us just stood there in the middle of the room. Something didn't feel right, there was an awkwardness about the whole thing. None of us were saying anything so eventually to break the silence, I said, 'I've just boiled the kettle'. So we had a cup of tea together. Eventually he asked all the things you'd expect a doctor to ask, you know, how are you feeling and so on. I didn't have any idea what was going on in his mind but I knew if I waited long enough he'd come out with it.

Eventually, and don't ask me how, we got round to my age and he asked me how old I was. I told him and he said, 'Are you sure?' I ought to know how old I am, I said. Then he opened his brief-case and took out my file. Well I might be a couple of years out, I said.

He told me he wanted me to have a test. What sort of a test? 'An amniocentesis,' he said, and what's that when it's at home, I thought, but before I had chance to ask him he explained it to me. They draw fluid from the womb. I was considered a high risk apparently because of my age and previous history. I didn't have to have it, but if I was asking his professional opinion, which I wasn't, he would strongly advise it. I want his baby, I said. I want it more than I want anything, and he could see I meant it. He put his hand on my shoulder and told me not to worry.

I didn't have to wait long. In fact I think my appointment came the following week. It wasn't a very pleasant thing to have done but it turned out that was the easy part.

A slight pause

He could only advise me. At the end of the end the final decision was mine.

A slight pause

I wrestled with it for days. I must have asked myself a million questions... the problem was I didn't have a million answers. All I knew for sure was that I was uncertain. I wanted this child for lots of reason... but the thought of bringing up another 'Downs'... I wanted someone in his image... someone who would grow up and would remind me of him, but I knew that one little extra chromosome was going to bugger all that up.

The situation was different to this as to when Linda was born. I had held her in my arms before I knew anything was wrong, you see. There was no such thing as an 'amniocentesis' in those days. It wouldn't have made any difference if there was, I know in my heart I would have still kept her.

A slight pause

That's what made it difficult for me the second time. I was completely torn. There I was on the one hand, desperately wanting something to hang on to, but knowing on the other if I'd kept it, it would mar the image of someone I held so very high...

Her words run out. Suddenly she comes back with renewed energy.

And it wouldn't have matter what I would have, a little boy or girl, all they would be in my eyes is the equivalent of that little petal that happened to be at the corner of Carlton's mouth when the shot was taken. Nature's little hand in the scheme of things.

Pause

When I worked it all out and realised I wanted the baby for totally selfish reasons it made it easier for me to come to a decision. Having it taken away was just like tearing up the photograph I told myself.

A slight pause

I don't know who I thought I was kidding. Oh I might have destroyed the photograph but the negative was up here.

She points to her head

It still is. That's the trouble, isn't it? We can go from day to day destroying as many pictures as we like... we still go round with our own personal album, and whenever we're lonely, or depressed or both out it comes... and when we do, we either think about whatever it is or we talk about it. And it doesn't matter if there's no-one there to listen. You see, I know I talk to myself. I'm not under any misapprehension there, but as far as I'm concerned it's all right because I know I don't do it in the company of others. I mean what would be the point?

Pause

I was admitted to hospital at ten a.m. on the sixth of August and I was back home by lunch-time on the seventh. The actual termination took less that a second. Less than a second... and the rest of my life. I'm still not over it. What was it I said earlier? A mother never gets over the death of a child and that's what it was, a child.

A slight pause

Although I knew this time I couldn't keep it, it's been difficult for me to live with the decision not to ever since. Difficult? I've attempted suicide twice. Oh yes... if it wasn't for the veggies across the way I wouldn't be here now.

I don't want to give the impression that the reason for it was solely my termination, far from it. There's never one reason for something like that, and I had a score of them. And it wasn't a conscious decision to end it all either. For me it was a natural progression of the way my life was going.

A slight pause

Quite by chance Fabian knocked my door and couldn't get an answer. He said afterwards he knew I was in because he happened to be looking out of his window and saw me draw my curtains closed. After breaking in he called Lorraine and it was she who sent for the ambulance.

When they pumped my stomach and knew I was going to be all right they transferred me to another part of the hospital. They kept me there for a month. I don't know how I stood it.

As soon as I came out they assigned me to a social worker. Charlotte. Nice girl, very young.

I don't know what it is about those people, but they're always looking for a reason for everything even when there isn't one. Half the time I make one up just to please her. I've been with her for a couple of years now. Idwal is on her books as well, and I'm not sure, but I think there's a few more here in the block too. When she comes to call she's in the building most of the day, I know that.

A slight pause

It used to be an offence, you know... attempting suicide. I didn't know that.

A slight pause

The second time I tried I almost got away with it, or almost didn't get away with it, depends on how you look at it.

It was a Tuesday which was something I wasn't aware of a the time. I was so deep in depression I wasn't aware of anything in those days let alone what day it was.

There was a very nice man who used to come round in a yellow van selling fish. I used to treat myself every week to a cutlet of hake... only this week he didn't have any. He explained apologetically then tried to palm me off with cod or whiting or something or other, but I wasn't having any of it. Apparently I made a terrible scene, at the end of which I'm told I stood at the side of his van in the pouring rain and cried like a child until eventually he realised he couldn't do anything with me and drove away.

It was... crazy. I knew it was only a piece of fish and wasn't that important but the whole thing just got to me. Nothing was trivial to me in those days.

A slight pause

When I got back inside the house it obsessed me.

Shouting

Why didn't he keep me my fish? He knows I have it every week. How would he like it if he kept it for me one week and I turned round and asked for something different? He doesn't like me, that's what it is, I thought... but why doesn't he like me, I haven't done anything to him. I thought the whole world was against me at that point.

A slight pause

That's when it started... 'thinking aloud'. That's the acceptable word for 'talking to yourself'.

When Charlotte came to see me in hospital the following day she couldn't understand why I had attempted it a second time. I was doing so well, she said. She didn't know the half. I'd never told her anything very much and I didn't intend starting now. I didn't tell her, but all I could think of that day was, one, I couldn't have my fish, two, I didn't have a husband, three, I'd buried my little girl, four, I probably was never going to set eyes on Carlton again, and five, I had had taken from me the only real chance I would ever have of knowing any real happiness... I had all that together with about fifty thousand other things flying around in my head at the same time. I just didn't want to go on anymore !

A pause

It was dark, and it was still raining and I wasn't wearing a coat. I knew that because when I was eventually discharged from hospital I didn't have one.

The only way I can describe how I was feeling that night was to liken it to how I imagine it would be to be hypnotised. I was aware of what I was doing and where I was going but everything seemed out of my hands... I was just going along with the flow.

A slight pause

It was foggy, and I remember I was staring down the track, waiting for the lights of the next valley sprinter. I was standing in the middle of the old wooden railway bridge. They've taken it down now, it was a favourite with suicides.

A slight pause

Because of the weather conditions I knew I'd have to be quick. The chances were, by the time I saw the lights through the fog, I wouldn't have time to climb the side and balance myself before jumping.

A slight pause

I needn't have worried. It was a disaster. I've accepted the fact now that it just wasn't meant to be, but I couldn't understand at first what had gone wrong. I could see the headlights of the train approaching about three hundred yards away. I got into position in plenty of time, closed my eyes and jumped.

A slight pause

You can imagine my surprise when I came round in hospital later with concussion, three squashed vertebrae and a fractured jaw.

A slight pause

I was told afterwards that I was very lucky. Instead of landing under the damned thing I ended up prostrate alongside it.

A slight pause

I can't say I haven't thought about doing it again since because I have. The truth is the idea is never far away... it crosses my mind most days... and nights. But I seem to cope. I've developed little ways to help me... and of course there's the Gamanil. They're an anti-depressant and I suppose they help. I'm given a week's supply at a time. I shan't have them for a longer period because they're considered a dangerous drug and I'm not to be trusted with large amounts.

On good days I try and go without and do, often.

Smiling

I've saved up about twenty over the months so there's not a problem now if I fancy having another try. I know I've used tablets before but believe me I've had it with trains.

A slight pause

My first attempt was kept rather quiet, but I was the talk of the place after the railway fiasco... it wasn't the first time I'd been talked about, I've always been good material in that respect. It started when Linda was born, continued when Ted left, I stirred a chorus of tongues wagging when John moved in and now there's the court case. God knows what I'd be labelled if they knew about Carlton.

A slight pause

Although he played his part in my downfall, it's only because of him I go on. Sometimes my head's like a seesaw with him at one end and Linda at the other. I want to be with both and can't be with either. Linda's part of why I want to go and he's only why I want to stay.

A slight pause

Everybody has to have one... a Carlton... a Mickey Mouse, there nothing odd about it. They're only 'reasons' and no-one survives without them.

A slight pause

When I was a little girl I had a raggy doll. I used to take it to bed every night and snuggle up to it. It was a great comfort to me.

A slight pause

The part of me that needed this is still there. You grow up, your body changes but some things stay the same.

A slight pause

When I go to bed at night I lay a pillow alongside of me, I know it's not him... but imagination is a wonderful thing. I see him, feel him... and I don't care about anything else because as far as I'm concerned he's laying next to me and that's all that matters.

The days I cope with the Gamanil... but the nights are harder sometimes.

Taking a bottle of aftershave from under the pillow

When all else fails I bring out the after-shave...

She sprays it in the air

... and I smell him. He always smelled so...

She doesn't finish the sentence. She puts the bottle to her nose and breathes in.

I asked him what it was, he told me and I bought him a bottle but

I never got round to giving it to him.

A slight pause as she puts the bottle down on the bed

On a bad day I've known me wear it and it's like he's in the same room as me. Once, I began to panic because I started spraying it on the pillow and I didn't realise until it was down to the half. I sent the empty box to a chemist in Cardiff and he managed to find a supplier so it's not a problem anymore. I rely on it so much I ought to be able to get it on prescription. I couldn't survive without it, I know that.

A slight pause

I hide the Gamanil in here.

She takes a vase and puts the palm of her hand over the top of it. She turns the vase upside down, then holds it away from her revealing a handful of tablets

I've decided if they send me down I'm definitely having a third attempt.

During the following she puts down the tablets and begins to separate them by moving them one by one from left to right.

Charlotte's convinced it won't come to that but no-one knows for sure. I can't face prison, I just can't... and I still believe in my heart of hearts I didn't do anything terribly wrong.

Charlotte says everything will be all right as long as I tell the judge exactly how it happened, but I don't know how it happened. All I remember is coming out of the chemist and looking into the pram.

A slight pause

He must have been about five or six months old. I looked down at him and there he was... dark skinned, dark hair... the image of Carlton. I leaned towards him and he smiled at me, he did, he really smiled at me.

A slight pause

I picked him up and kissed him on the head... he smelled so beautiful too. He kept smiling and didn't take his eyes off me. I was so intent on making cooing noises I barely heard his mother scream. When I did look up she was across the road... or rather I was. As God is my judge I don't remember crossing it. She was hysterical now and screaming for her baby. 'It's all right,' I shouted, 'Don't panic, he's over here with me.' I crossed the road and she immediately snatched him back. I apologised but there was quite a crowd around by this time. A policeman appeared and the next thing I knew I was taken in for questioning.

A slight pause

I don't know how long afterwards, but Charlotte turned up and she eventually took me home. The good thing about it she kept telling me was that I crossed the road and gave the baby back... but what bothers me is I don't remember crossing it in the first place, and if I can't explain it to myself how am I going to explain it to a judge?

A slight pause

Sometimes I think I've worked everything out... but the feeling doesn't last very long. It's all still a mess and stands every chance of becoming worse.

It's at times like this...

A slight pause

Sometimes I don't see any way out. Charlotte says that when I feel like that I'm to get in touch. It doesn't matter when, day or night... I don't think she'd appreciate me ringing her up now, do you? The last thing I'd want is to get a call from someone on New Year's Eve letting me know that they're seriously considering suicide.

A slight pause

Am I seriously considering it? I suppose I am really.

A slight pause

My case comes up on the second... tomorrow.

Another slight pause. She has now finished counting the tablets.

Twenty-seven. More than I thought. More than enough too I imagine.

I haven't worked out how I'm going to do it yet, but I've got to think of a way of hiding them on me so that if the worst happens in court all I have to do is ask to use the bathroom.

A slight pause

I could do it before then of course...

She looks down at the tablets

... but not tonight, I think. I'm sorry Linda but good old Carlton wins again.

She returns the tablets to the vase and makes her way towards the bed

It's not impossible I suppose that he could be in the country... may even be standing at the end of the street waiting to pluck up enough courage to come and knock on my door.

She smiles to herself

I told you imagination is a wonderful thing.

With renewed gusto

It doesn't matter where he is anyway because in a minute or two he's going to be right here with me.

She positions one of the pillows vertically on the bed

It won't be long now before I can put out the light, close my eyes and we can snuggle up together.

She takes the bottle of aftershave and sprays it on the pillow

Perfect.

Replacing the bottle under the pillow

All right, Carlton, I won't be a minute.

She goes back to the living area where she switches off a light. Now only the lights on the Christmas tree are on. She takes a wet-wipe and quickly cleans her face.

I'm almost ready. Did you have a nice flight? I appreciate you're jet-lagged, but I hope you're not going to go to sleep on me straight away, are you? There's a million things I want to ask you. I'm amazed you found me. I haven't always lived here you know. I lived in a far nicer house than this.

She is now standing at the side of the bed looking down at the pillow

You haven't changed, you know.

A slight pause

Smile for me?

Presumably he does because she gives a huge smile back. Her smile is interrupted though by a knock on the front door. The fantasy is broken immediately. She is slightly panicked.

Who on earth is that?

After quickly thinking about it

Kids probably. I'm not going to answer it.

A slight pause

I'm not usually wished a Happy New Year.

A slight pause

What if it's not kids? What if it's him... Carlton.

The door is knocked again

Wouldn't it be just my luck to have him knock and me not answer?

Telling herself

It's ridiculous, it's not him... it never is... but I just can't take the chance.

Back to the fantasy

No, don't get out of bed. I'm just going to answer that and I'll be straight back with you... keep it warm for me.

She leaves to answer the door. It's knocked again. She calls

Just a minute. I'm coming, I'm coming.

Eileen leaves the room. We hear the sound of one or maybe two locks being unbolted.

Oohh Fabian, it's you. I'm sorry I can't ask you in... it's not convenient. You see... I have a visitor staying... from America.

Suddenly the opening bars of 'When You Wish Upon A Star' is heard. Cross fade to the vocals of the last verse, 'Like a bolt out of the blue, fate steps in and sees you through,' Play to the end of the song. The lights fade leaving a coloured shaft of light shining on the bed.

Stories, Subjects and Identities

David Adams

I concluded my Foreword by asking who, in these five plays, was saying what, to whom, how were they saying it - and why. What I want to explore here is how these monodramas deal with 'reality' by examining in more detail how their characters see it - and what significance this has for us, as an audience or readers. All texts are *representations*, of course, offering a version of reality in a cultural form, but the monodrama, we have established, is a unique discourse: it is, here, one man's voice mediated by the character and (absent) actor that is exclusively concerned with themselves and their world - what's called today *personhood*. How, then, do these five stories represent explorations of personhood?

Mark Jenkins's *Playing Burton* has been a huge hit, with around 400 performances since it was first produced in 1991. Taken up by director Guy Masterson, with Josh Richards playing Burton, it has played in Wales (including Burton's home town, Port Talbot), London, New York, Edinburgh, Budapest, Jerusalem and Hong Kong. As I write it is about to tour the USA.

The reviews were, and still are, uniformly enthusiastic. But they are also interesting. 'The legend is given his own voice,' said the *Western Mail*. 'Jenkins reveals with authenticity Burton's innermost thoughts,' opined *The Stage*. 'Allowing an almost voyeuristic insight,' commented the *Liverpool Echo*. Somehow Mark Jenkins was deemed to have literally re-created Richard Burton, as if he had special access to the deceased actor's mind, body and spirit, in a truly postmodernist confusion of reality and fiction. The playwright bestows the gift of speech ('given his own voice') on the mythical person - the dramatist as Creator; he 'reveals' what this once-real person (but here, let's remember, a dramatic character in a play) was thinking but never actually said - the dramatist as spiritual medium; the playwright allows the audience to know things that they are not supposed to know, a voyeuristic insight - the dramatist as webcam. True to the heavy hint in the title, *Playing* Burton, this is a monodrama about role-play, about the Pirandellian problems of actor, character, persona, rather than a biography or character-study.

As with so many biodramas (such as Sian Phillips's *Marlene*, which unfortunately never really got beyond impersonation) what's fascinating is this inseparability of reality and fiction. We see variations on the theme in such diverse forms as TV soaps and the media obsession with their actors/characters, *Schindler's List*, *The Truman Story*, Ali G and *Big Brother*. Ted John, Alex, Eileen and Lee are all dramatic fictions who may or may not be modelled on real people, but the character 'Richard Burton' in *Playing Burton* is Richard Burton - to most. The role of author is acknowledged - but more as exhumer, facilitator, spirit voice, revealer of secrets, broadcaster of hitherto unrevealed archive footage. He is simply the medium through which the *ur*-Burton expresses what he didn't get round to when he was alive.

None of our five 'voices' are simple, and Burton is as complex, or fractured, as the rest, being at least two characters in one - miner's son Richard Jenkins, Jenks, the original, and Richard Burton, the actor, the role Jenks lives to play. And Burton himself becomes the roles he has to play - Faust, Antony, Macbeth, Hamlet, Prince Hal, King Arthur, George, Alec Leamass, Churchill, O'Neill, as much as the larger-than-life personality created by his publicists and the media. Playing Burton (the task, not the title) was a problematic job for the person who still liked to call himself Jenks, lurching from fictional character to fictional character, including the composite one known as Burton.

Some parts Burton himself realises are intermingled with his own identity. Mark Jenkins (the playwright, no relation to his subject) has around thirty quotations peppered throughout the script (that's more than one a page), with more from Marlowe's *Dr Faustus* than any other, so he presumbly sees Burton as obsessed by the story of the man who sold his soul to the Devil - but what was the Devil? Hollywood? Fame? Drink? Burton also realises that Edward Albee's dysfunctional couple in *Who's Afraid of Virginia Woolf* was too close for comfort: 'Are we Richard and Elizabeth playing George and Martha? Or are we, my God it can't be … are we George and Martha playing Richard and Elizabeth? The lines remember me; the play interprets us…' Life imitating art or art imitating life? But he is also Alec, the spy who came in from the cold in the film of Le Carre's novel: 'I have an image in my mind. It is of a man perched on top of a wall. If he drops down on one side, he's made the last choice he will ever make. He denies himself all other options. He takes his place in an ordered, puritanical Utopia …on the other side lies an uncertain world, where he free to squander his talents or succeed …but most of all …to generally make a fool of himself …' And the last role he recalls is his final one, O'Neill, the man from the Ministry of Truth in *1984*, telling Winston Smith: 'No-one who has gone astray is ever spared. And even if we chose to let you live out the natural term of your life, you still would never escape us … never again will you be capable of love, or friendship, or joy of living, laughter, or curiosity, or courage, or integrity. You will be hollow …we shall squeeze you empty… And then we shall fill you with ourselves'. And Burton asks himself 'Could it be possible, I wonder, ever to do that? Completely drain a man of his identity and create a totally new one? Well, actors try… But how much of you survives?' At the end of the play the working-class Welshman that was once Richard Jenkins does indeed seem to have been replaced by an invented representational character called Richard Burton.

Mark Jenkins wrote *Playing Burton* just after the actor's death in 1984 (commissioned, ironically, by a Welsh actor who never played the part), so the monodrama has its roots in hagiography or at least biography. It transcends the genre by becoming a study of not just the classic actor's existentialist dilemma (as in Sartre's *Keane*) but of fractured identity - in both the man and the culture.

* * * *

Envy was originally written by Edward Thomas in 1993 as the first of a series on the Seven Sins; the other six remain a tantalisingly unfulfilled project. It is a misleading title, perhaps, because the play isn't so much about envy as delusion, fantasy, failure, revenge even. It is not envy that drives Ted John to put himself forward as a Mastermind contestant - it is a bizarrely misplaced sense of self-worth and a desire to please his mother. It is not really envy that makes him kidnap the successful local big noise who does get invited to appear on the quiz show - it is resentment. And it is not envy that makes him stage his surreal version of the TV show, complete with imitation Magnus Magnusson and painted audience, in the welfare hall - it is the need to make his fiction come true.

Be that as it may, *Envy* was superbly realised by Y Cwmni, (later renamed Fiction Factory) Thomas's company, with Russell Gomer (for whom it was written) as Ted John, although it never really saw major success. One suspects if it had been at Edinburgh it would have become a cult hit, but it was performed sporadically, revived for the 1995 Cardiff Summer Festival and redrafted by the author as a screenplay in 1999.

The themes, the characters and the setting are all familiar to anyone who has seen Ed Thomas's work, all based on the author's own life. Ted John (whose preferred nickname, Scon, also appears in *East From the Gantry*) is a loner from Cwmgiedd - the real by-passed town which was Thomas's home that also appears in *East From the Gantry* and *Song from a Forgotten City*. The darts match in the Drum and Monkey is recounted elsewhere, in *Flowers of the Dead Red Sea*, and other incidents pop up throughout Thomas's oeuvre. Sid Lewis, the local hero who becomes Ted John's victim, is the name of the main character in *House of America*. Ron pops up elsewhere, as both an uncle (as here) and as the eccentric dreamer of *East From the Gantry*. Telly Savalas, as well as Magnus Magnussen and Fred Housego, are also referred to in other plays. Mickey Jones, the butcher's son who brings a troupe of actors back to shock the town, is obviously Thomas himself, the son of the town butcher and director/writer of Y Cwmni.

Cwmgiedd is, in some ways, the Llaregyb of that other Thomas's *Under Milk Wood*. We meet, albeit fleetingly, the Rev David Davies and his wife Edna, garage owner Vic Small and son Harry, illicit lover of Mrs Davies, Jim Lewis, Haydn and Moira Griffiths, Mickey Batts, Sgt Perkins, Glan Price, Harry Gwynn, Clive from the bank, John and Edna Hickey, Beti Webb, Freddie Jones, Sid Lewis and his wife Ang, his father Glyn, and the kids as well as Evvie, Ted's widowed mother, and her brother, his Uncle Ron. We can't help feeling that the author has put just about all his friends' names in *Envy*. The anti-hero, Ted, we get to know well: nearly 30, unmarried, lives on his own, father died when he was six, brought up by an ageing mother and a morbid uncle obsessed with disasters (who, incidentally, in Russell Gomer's portrayal, causes the nervy Ted to twitch at the mention of his name as if there were the repressed memory of some childhood abuse). Ted has a special relationship with his mother, inevitably, and to an extent it is only for her that he wants to win Mastermind - even after she has died he wants to present her with the trophy as a bowl for her Turkish Delights.[5]

The motivation is not simply oedipal. Ted sees himself as a saviour. The village hall is the heart and soul of the community and by glorifying Cwmgiedd's miners' welfare hall, Ted is defending the spirit of Wales itself. Convinced because he knows the history of the hall he is a Mastermind, he represents a nation that fools itself into believing that by living on memory it is somehow superior. Sid Lewis becomes merely the bourgeois *arriviste*.

Ted is a sad character who misreads everything and exists as just that - a recognisably pathetic psychopath - but also as a metaphor for the nation. The degree of pessimistic cultural self-loathing is striking even in the context of Thomas's work around this period.

* * * *

If Ted John is an outsider whose story is both a personal confession and a cultural critique, then he has his match in Ian Rowlands's Alex - another outsider who thinks he can create a way out of his individual and social dilemma. *A Marriage of Convenience* is regarded by many as Ian Rowlands's best play. Others see it as a fine piece of writing, but more a short story or perhaps a radio play. [6]

It is set on the wedding day of Prince Charles and Lady Diana Spencer, July 29 1991 (when the hero, Alex, is apparently 18), but was actually produced in 1996, and again in 1997, when it was supported by the *Yes for Wales* campaign, which wished Rowlands' company Theatr y Byd every success and encouraged the audience to vote YES in the forthcoming referendum. Interestingly, it was originally conceived as a four-hander and was rewritten virtually overnight because of financial constraints; however it has had three major tours, won an Angel, earned the actor Gareth Potter a *Stage* nomination for Best Actor at Edinburgh and won a Best Production award at the Dublin Festival.

Essentially the play takes the form of a young man, Alex, telling us about his unsatisfactory search for a personal identity that is rooted in his Welshness. It takes us from his unhappy experience at a Welsh-language school in the predominantly anglophone

Rhondda Valley (where he was sent at his since-deceased father's behest) to his acceptance (thanks to a non-dogmatic West Walian friend's family) that language was but 'one strand in a broader politic'. At the same time he tells a more domestic story, that of his troubled relationship with his mother and step-father, resulting in his displacing the abusive interloper.

Two basic metaphors run through the monodrama: the union, or marriage of the title, and mountains/valleys. Rowlands shows elsewhere he is interested in how the power balance in larger political situations (notably imperialism and patriarchy) is paralleled in those in personal relationships. As England dominates Wales (and its other colonies), so men have dominated women, goes the analogy.[7] The Act of Union was a marriage of convenience, like the union of Charles and Diana, like the relationship between Alex's mother and stepfather in *Marriage of Convenience*, like the possibility of Alex's relationship with Wendy, like the 'marriage' (Alex's word) between the Welsh language and South-East Wales, 'a region that had long forgotten the sound of its own past'.

While the notion of the unequal and pragmatic relationship is one theme clearly present in the text, the idea of relative levels was more manifest when the drama was staged - the set was little more than a ramp. The idea of ascending into enlightenment is a commonplace idea, of course, from Plato's allegory of the cave to countless pop songs; but Rowlands does give it a lyricism and offers some variations. Down in the valley the plebs unthinkingly celebrate the Royal Wedding, Alex's mother tolerates the boorishness of her new partner, Wendy's family live in their MFI-furnished terraced house; up in the hills the Welsh nationalists have their own picnic, the air is cleaner and Alex remembers going walking with his father on Snowdon. Down below there is darkness, on high there is light; down there is ignorance, up here there is knowledge. Alex is forever striving to climb out of his slough of despair. 'Faced with mountains, we have to climb them,' a voice-over announces at the beginning. 'What else can we do bar scramble out of the dark and into the light, it's instinctive for a kid born in the shade to strive for the sun.' And again it is the voice-over (the author?) which ends the monodrama: 'Born in the valley we can never truly escape it, though we may rise to the brim and glimpse freedom promised in a beam of light, we are allowed only instants of hope before sliding back under the weight of our legacy, back into the pit where all pits have been and gone. But we still climb on, because in our moments of light lie our reasons for living.'

You don't need to be a committed Freudian to recognise some possible interpretations here. This is basically the story of Oedipus: a son is taken to a hillside, brought up by strangers and returns years later; he is in love with his mother and wants to destroy his rival, her husband; he goes with guilt and confusion into exile, doomed to wander the world blind. Alex naturally has yet to slay the Theban Sphinx and free his country from oppression, although, of course, he does defeat and expel his stepfather. It is not difficult to look beyond the oedipal ambivalence recognised by Alex to see the whole process of sublimation and transference. Alex's conflicting feelings about his mother (and mother is the Valleys and also the matriarchal early world of the Imaginary) and the loss of his father (not only absent authority but the later patriarchal ordered world of the Symbolic) are sublimated into his political desires, his quest for true nationalism.

Is Alex's fascination with nationalism, then, simply a product of his domestic dissatisfaction, if not his oedipal fixation? Is his desire to climb the heights a rejection of his working-class values? Why does he associate his dead father with Snowdon, and hence higher aspirations? What do we make of the ambivalence toward his mother, where guilt, belonging, love, contempt, all make it more than oedipal? Does his mother stand for vulgarity, the Valleys, ignorance? Is there in all this not only a sexism but an elitism, a supremacism even, which might be associated with nationalism? Highs and lows, we might also remind ourselves, are the symptoms of manic depression; the geographic extremes may not only be a metaphor for spiritual and intellectual extremes but may express, albeit unwittingly, a bipolar disorder in Alex. They also signify the binary opposites that create meaning - and peg it to a gender, with the father here associated with heights, the mother with depths. These are confusing and confused issues that only a detailed psychological reading of the play could help elucidate. What does emerge strongly from re-encountering the play on the page is the complexity, the interplay between overt and covert themes, between the intended and the interpreted, between the fictional and the autobiographical, between representation and reality.

* * * *

Roger Williams is the youngest of the five dramatists represented in this volume.[5] *Saturday Night Forever* is a basic love story, told in the breathless style of teenage romances, and if it were a boy-meets-girl narrative it would be utterly trite - but if it were, and this is precisely the point, it would not end in tragedy.

Williams's voice here, Lee, is almost an anti-hero, but unlike Ted John he is simply *not heroic* in that he is disarmingly naïve and ordinary. He is set up as so uncluttered as to be instantly likeable - a recognisable person who happens to be gay. Indeed, Lee's concerns and lifestyle can seem trivial and petty. He is still slightly bedazzled by the attractions of clubs where the issues revolve around the quality of boy bands and the durability of Abba. Lee creates his personality for us in terms of his taste: doesn't like Take That, Titanic, Steps, Spcie Girls, Celine Dion, Habitat, Bacardi Breezers.

The title, of course, is a parody of the discomanic (and ultra heterosexual) John Travolta classic 1977 movie *Saturday Night Fever*. Lee, however, is no dance-floor star - indeed, he can't dance at all. His alter-ego, Matthew, does and represents the stereotypical clubber: he dines on fish fingers and spaghetti, drinks at gay bars, consumes TV like many other young people - *Big Break* and *Blind Date* as a pleasant brain-numbing prelude to a night out - and shops in Barker, Floyd, Westworld, French Connection, Gap. For this is not Seventies Brooklyn, but Cardiff in the late 1990s.

Saturday Night Forever is an insidious product: not only does it have that massive sting in the tail, it seduces the audience into seeing the plot as a cheap romance. Williams appropriates and then subverts the love-story genre with quite delicious irony. We know nothing about Lee other than his high-hormone emotional life - what he does for a living, what serious things he thinks about, what he likes (as opposed to what he doesn't like), all is unrevealed. He exists only as a first-person narrator of a story that is mind-bogglingly unexceptional until the climax. He thinks and talks in the cliches of the genre: 'Carl was a nice man. We'd had a great conversation during which I'd deluded myself that we would've made a great couple. Somewhere in my fantasy world I'd even picked out a colour scheme for our living room. Burnt oranges and reds if you must know....'

The point is that someone who falls head over heels in love in a straight boy-girly romance will live happily ever after... To have two people who just wanted to be in love - a trite, even mawkish story - yet have someone die because of it, is familiar through classical romantic tragedy like *Romeo and Juliet*. *Saturday Night Forever* is deliberately unclassically low-cultured - but it contains within it the same indictment of society's intolerance of *difference*. Being different is not easy, an unselfconsciously 'out' gay Lee learns.

Reading *Saturday Night Forever*, it is difficult to appreciate the impact the play has in performance: here (and specifically in a Wales where gayness is notoriously invisible and macho lads' culture rules) was an explicit story of homosexual love told with disarming ingenuousness and candour. For any audience, it's a shock. For a gay audience, it is a very big deal.

What Williams does effectively is to replace the conventional phallocentric perspective with what's been called 'the homosexual gaze'.[9] He makes the gay experience central and in so doing makes an important statement of self-affirmation. It is significant, too, that he insists on having signed performances (interpreted into British Sign Language): issues of inclusion and minorities are important to him. His writing is also very accessible, drawing in an audience who may not be interested in sexual politics.

* * * *

Sleeping With Mickey stands out from the rest of the monodramas here because although it is 'one man's voice' - that of Frank Vickery - in terms of authorship, the voice used by the narrator is that of a woman. Nothing that unusual - Willie Russell and Alan Bennett have had great success with one-woman plays - but particular issues of gender discourse do arise here. Whose voice are we hearing - a man's or a woman's?

Vickery has always been good at creating female roles and in his professional career as a playwright he has written several specially for the experienced Swansea actress Menna Trussler - including *Sleeping with Mickey*, which was written between his enormously successful *A Kiss on the Bottom* and its rather less successful follow-up, *Loose Ends*, both featuring Marlene, a larger-than-life cancer survivor. Commissioned by Phil Clark at the Sherman Theatre, Cardiff, *Sleeping with Mickey* opened in the Arena, the Sherman studio space, in July 1992 before going on to The Grand, Swansea. It was subsequently adapted as a half-hour television drama, in a highly acclaimed production starring Brenda Blethyn.[10]

The play is structured around New Year 1988-9, with the

first act leading up to midnight, the second act afterwards. The two halves are deliberately different in tone as it leaps from poignant comedy to dark near-tragedy. Like all our other 'voices' Eileen is a loner, someone whose life has fallen apart. The mother of a Down's Syndrome daughter, she suffers a deserting husband, an unconsummated non-affair with a married man, the death of her child, a brief but passionately physical holiday relationship and a breakdown in her mental health leading to suicide attempts and a court case - all this from a writer best known for farce!

The play, then, gets increasingly black, moving from presenting Eileen as an amusing, confident figure sure of her views (on television to vegetarianism) to one who is revealed as damaged, relying on fantasy, not really knowing reality from fiction. Her one positive experience was a fling with an American called Carlton just after her daughter's death when she treated herself to a holiday in Disney World [11]. She welcomes the resulting pregnancy, seeing a child as proof of her affair and a replication of her lover Carlton, until she is told that the child would be Down's Syndrome and therefore reluctantly agrees to a termination. Only when we get to near the end of the piece do we have the information to understand her dilemma - that she is facing an appearance in court the next day on a charge of baby-stealing.

To an extent the play is (like *Envy*) about memory, how it is constructed and used. For Eileen, her history is one determined by ill-luck. 'Funny how life has a way of dealing you a card from the bottom of the deck, though, isn't it,' she muses (though attributing the thought to her husband). 'That's something I haven't enjoyed very much of, you know...luck' 'that old thing called 'luck' popped its ugly little head up again' 'Nothing ever goes the way you expect it to though, does it?' A malevolent Fate steps in all too often: 'They say everything has a reason...' 'It's a strange old world..' 'I took it as a sign' 'if nature hadn't stepped in...' 'I've accepted the fact now that it just wasn't meant to be...' And who can blame her? As she channel-hops on her expensive big-screen Nicam stereo television, her very first words to us set the agenda: 'Pathetic, isn't it?' she complains. 'What's my choice?' Life, like TV, seems already programmed by a higher authority.

But it isn't simple destiny. As we listen to Eileen's story and feel increasingly sympathetic to this woman who has no control over her life we might acknowledge an alternative, hidden, narrative. What she tells us is of course her own story and is necessarily subjective - but where does reality end and fantasy take over? Eileen's memory is selective: she can delete or invent but also be amazingly precise about, for example, dates - she tells us that her daughter Linda was born on Independence Day 1954, lived 28 years and has been dead now for six years, which sets the present the turn of the year 1988-9. That makes Eileen no younger than around 55 - and the fact (as she tells us) she can remember seeing a film made in 1942 six times means she is probably nearer 60, yet she vaguely describes herself as 'knocking 40' when she met Carlton five years previously and, slightly more honestly, fifty-something now.

The vagueness (emphasised by the stage directions) may start as a jokey feminine embarrassment but the very precision of the chronology detailed means we can work out pretty soon that this could be more a signal of escape from reality. Did John, the teacher who lodged with her after her husband deserted them, give her any sustenance to allow her to imagine they might have been lovers, or was it wishful thinking? Did the caring vegetarian couple across the road really offer her cold broccoli and nut sandwiches? It's presented as no more than a joke to show her as rather humorous, conservative but tolerant, but it does also reveal a tendency, perhaps, to invent.

Crucially, what is invented about her memory of the crucial moment in her life? During a holiday in Disneyland she is courted by the hotel waiter, Carlton, by her description a strikingly attractive young man of immaculate appearance, who eventually (she tells us) makes love to her repeatedly, leading her to question, understandably, if it was a dream. The last she sees of him (at least she assumes it's him) is his waving goodbye dressed in a Mickey Mouse costume in his other job at Disney World. From then on he obsesses her - and her grasp on reality loosens completely. After all, she thinks, she experienced the conflation of reality and fantasy: a love affair with a handsome and very virile young man who leads another life as a fictional ridiculous cartoon character in the make-believe world of Disneyland.

Fact and fiction were one in Carlton and from then on Eileen has problems discerning truth and fantasy. Reality strikes in the form of a foetus, the result of her afternoon of sex in Disney World. After the abortion she has a breakdown and now lives in sheltered accommodation (though she seems not to realise it). She makes two attempts at suicide, having hidden away the pills ready for a third, and has no recollection of the incident when she took a baby from its pram.

It is an immensely sad tale, told with immense sympathy by Vickery. The issue of baby-snatching achieved some publicity in the late 1980s and one can imagine the starting-point for this drama being the question of why might a woman commit this act. Eileen is convincingly portrayed as sympathetic to others' flaws: she does not criticise her husband for walking out when Linda is born, she suggests that it was high-minded fidelity to his wife that made John fail to consummate their unspoken love, she is convinced Carlton was a gentleman who only made love to her because she called him back [12]. But we are hearing this version of a pathetic life from someone who has lost their grip on reality. Her experience, up to Disney World, is utterly credible. We believe her implicitly - until we realise she just might be fantasising. And in terms of the dramatic experience, we can engage with the play by accepting Eileen's version *and* by reading a parallel version that is only gradually revealed.

It is interesting to note that Vickery now spends most of his time writing television soaps. *Sleeping With Mickey* can be seen as a kind of soap, itself regarded as a female cultural form: soaps traditionally are about feeling, domestic issues, maternal responsibilities, rather than the male cultural signifiers of action, work, toughness, the public arena. This is theatre, of course, while soap drama is essentially a television serial form and Eileen's story is not altogether an everyday tale of everyday people - though it has an ordinariness and familiarity about it. The genre is subverted up to a point - the play has the idealised mother easily recognised by a soap audience, but here it is represented problematically. I suspect that while audiences in general have shown they can engage with *Sleeping with Mickey*, its 'ideal spectator', the audience addressed, is the female.[13] Eileen is not patronised and to a great extent she can be seen not as a victim but a survivor. Small wonder that so many female audiences find it difficult to accept that the role was created by a male author.

* * * *

What all five characters share, however different they may be, is a lack of confidence about who they are - their personhood. The very notion of identity is, these postmodernist days, problematic. Self-identity can no longer be seen simply as a collection of individual characteristics but a narrative we ourselves construct - and alter. These plays show us five people who seem to be using the monologue to tell us a story, about themselves, one which they themselves believe but which in at least one instance (*Envy*) we are meant to read differently.[14]

Each character on the surface does little more than tell us about themselves - theirs are subjective, narcissistic narratives, concerned with 'self' rather than 'the Other'[15]. But the Other is always present and it helps define the subject - Burton's Other is Jenks, the soul that the actor has lost (or sold); Ted John's is the invisible opponent Sid Lewis, succeeding where he didn't; Alex's is

England and the father, intertwined entities in his Freudian world; Lee's is the heterosexual male, an unacknowledged but powerful opponent; Eileen's is the absent fantasy lover Carlton and their aborted child. But they are subjects simply in that they tell us their narratives through the first person singular (the nominative voice) - *I*. The *I* gives an obviously selective viewpoint, the self. That self is inherently unstable, however: all the stories here are about characters, initially apparently so sure of themselves, so well-defined as persons, who collapse into fragile confusion. These monodramas offer pretty unreliable evidence.

Burton, Ted, Alex, Lee and Eileen are, as characters with their own subjective identities, also culturally constructed by the worlds they inhabit, just as all of us may be individuals but none of us is a free agent and is *subject* to ideologies and social forces. They are, then, also subjects in the sense that each of us is subject to something else. Each character is, of course, also constructed by their author and by us as readers finding our own meanings.[16]

Thus, in the most extreme case, we have Ted John deluding himself that by knowing the history of his welfare hall he can be a Mastermind champion, and the more he tells us about himself the more pathetic he becomes. Alex, with disarming honesty, exposes himself as a frustrated loner with an ambiguous relationship to his mother and an elitist social attitude and possible manic-depressive. Lee talks about his two lovers in a Mills-and-Boon style that allows us to see him as a naïve romantic while signalling that real life is a very different and a more serious business. Burton constantly refers (or defers) to Jenks, the 'real' person behind the persona that is Burton, caught in the classic dilemma of the performer as regards the relationship between person, actor and character. And Eileen, we ultimately realise, whose only meaningful experience is an affair with someone who doubles as Mickey Mouse, is telling us her story while under severe mental stress.

How do our five characters define themselves? How do any

of us define ourselves? By gender, by class, by race, by nationality. First, as noted in the Foreword, the dramatists are, of course, male and the characters are gendered. Burton desperately tries to define himself by the roles he has played professionally (dramatic characters and those demanded by fame and notoriety) and in terms of his masculinity, aggressively heterosexual, a victim of publicity about affairs, of vanity and desires; yet we know as a teenager he was adopted by an openly gay schoolteacher (whose surname he took) and he reacts defensively to the suggestion that his priapism might be rooted in repressed homosexuality. Ted John suffers from the absent-father syndrome, has no sexual experience but is possibly arrested at the infantile stage of sexual development. Alex is also oedipal and the only women we hear of are his mother and a sort-of girlfriend ('not in the top and bottom sense') both of whom he despises. Lee, ironically, seems oblivious to the social implications of being gay in a heterosexual culture until too late, and certainly has no concept of 'identity politics'; his view of other men is either romantic (if they're gay) or frightened (if they're macho-heterosexual). Eileen is on the surface almost saintly and certainly sees herself as the victim of circumstance - a rather particular creation of an idealised female from a particular male perspective.

Apart from *Sleeping with Mickey*, none of these monodramas feature women in a sympathetic light. Burton may have some regrets about his treatment of women, but we are presented with a very macho perspective. The general absence of women (or rather, only their presence as mothers) in the lives of Ted John and Alex is significant. The only female in Lee's life is a straight, tactless casual friend. Only Eileen is represented in a positive light - and even here there is that undertow that suggests she has invented some of her past.

How else do we define ourselves? By class, perhaps, and all our five characters are refreshingly working-class, sure if not necessarily happy in their social roots. Burton has escaped from manual toil with his original self, Jenks, as a reminder - symbolically it was the middle-class schoolmaster who 'rescued' him whose name the young actor assumes - and in his ascent into higher social class he tries to repress his origins, rejecting his name and his family, and in so doing contributes to his general loss of self-identity. Ted John cannot challenge the successful bourgeois Sid Lewis and is driven by frustration, resentment, misplaced pride and general impotence to destroy him and what he represents; it is a meaningless and futile act that changes nothing. Alex is continually trying to climb out of the abyss that is proletarian ignorance and collusion up into the heights of self-knowledge, yet finds that the air may be clearer but also more elitist: his is a battle to reconcile his roots and his aspirations. Lee lives in his own world, an ironic gay mirror-image of the macho Italian-American community, enjoying working-class pleasures, consuming working-class mass culture, his lack of awareness leading to his suffering from working-class homophobic violence: his life-style is that of an innocent hedonist and a mindless consumer. Eileen, perhaps, is working-class because that is the milieu her creator and his audience know, but she is also a conservative and a snob - ridiculing 'veggies', disdaining Splott - and will spend nearly £500 on both a holiday and on a television, though she has no discernible source of income). She seems working-class, indeed, not in terms of 'real' character but as a product of a genre which deals in working-class women.

The remaining area of self-identity is that of 'roots' - race, ethnicity and nationality. Where they come from is always important to our five characters - Burton's origins as Richard Jenkins in Pontrhydyfen haunt him; in Ted John's case, he seems to define himself to an extent in terms of the litany of names of residents in his home town; Alex too employs topographical detail to establish his own authenticity; Lee is a stranger from the sticks in a city he doesn't understand; Eileen is rooted in the Valleys, despite her slightly bourgeois airs. If this is ethnicity, it is very limited in geographical compass - *y filltir sgwar*. Nevertheless we must remember that while Burton, Ted and Alex to an extent conform to the disputed cultural concept of The Celt, the dramas also suggest the idea that to be Welsh is to be not-English, not-Scots, not-Irish, not-immigrant, leading to the disturbing idea of ethnic purity.

One interesting thing about Carlton is intriguingly ambiguous: was he black? Was Eileen, for all her working-class conservatism, 'colour blind'? Her description of Carlton is on the surface a romanticised matinee-idol list of attributes: turquoise eyes, black eyebrows and moustache, perfect nose, white teeth, immaculate hair, young and beautiful, a list which might also be attributed to a stereotypical gay man. When she recalls the baby she unconsciously snatched she says, 'there he was…dark skinned, dark hair … the image of Carlton'.[17] This is the nearest we get to a person of colour in these five plays. These are white, male, Welsh, narratives. If we do represent our worlds and create our self-identities partly in terms of race, ethnicity and nationality, then Welshness, or Welsh national and cultural identity, which we inevitably touch on again below, is a key representation in these monodramas. The absence of black and Asian people does not reflect the actual picture in Wales today (even less in Burton's 'not-Wales') but their invisibility implies that they are not seen as part of the Welsh nation and Welsh life.

Nationalism is problematic, of course, an endless debate in itself, and embraces issues of race and ethnicity, but 'national identity' can be seen as a device which unifies through suppression of *difference*. While Eileen's world, with its English and Americans, is reasonably inclusive (with her daughter she has had to cope, after all, with the 'threat of living with difference', as has Lee), Alex's, for example, explicitly excludes anyone who is not Welsh.

* * * *

I have already noted that all these first-person narratives seem to be about themselves, and no-one else, to the point of self-obsession. In fact every one of the five characters seems to have alienated themselves from society. They are outsiders. Burton has put himself beyond the pale because of his behaviour, his inability to reconcile the 'real' him, Jenks, and the public persona. Ted John knows everyone in the town but would appear to have no friends. Lee is gay - by definition (and self-definition) an outsider in a straight Cardiff scene - and suffers for it. Alex feels neither part of the 'high' Welsh-language nationalist coterie or the 'low' anglophone Valleys life. Eileen has become disconnected to everyone and everything - she not only has to give herself her own Christmas presents and talks to herself but has essentially lost contact with the 'real' world.[18] All five characters define themselves, then, by what they lack: identity would seem to be about absence as well as presence.

If we do define ourselves by what we are not as much as by what we are, by comparison, then all our five 'voices' have problems - identity crises. They are in this respect typical products of our postmodern condition.

All these are more than individual self-identities, though. Ted John's dissembling, his inferiority complex, his naïve overvaluing of the history of his welfare hall, his reliance on past glories, sad as they are, also constitute the created narrative of Welsh cultural identity. Ed Thomas, in plays like *House of America* and *East From the Gantry*, has explored that idea of the Welsh needing to reinvent themselves as a nation, the destructive nature of relying on myths and lies as defining cultural traits, the lack of self-esteem. Here Ted John embodies that false consciousness and is a metaphor for Wales. His self-identity is the same self-deluding narrative that makes up the cultural identity of Wales.

Burton is confused between the real person and his roles. But he also embodies the myth of the Welsh boyo, the working-class miner's son who becomes world-famous and hence, crucially, irresistible to beautiful women - a fantasy echoed by Tom Jones, of course, where the roots, the voice, the accent, the fame and the randiness are replayed in an almost ironic version. Burton's vain quest for his 'authentic' identity is bound up with Welshness, as we see in his references to his humble beginnings, his use of the Welsh language, his retention of 'Jenks' as his 'real' self.

In another allegorical narrative, Alex stumbles from early contacts with nationalism and a father who takes him up Snowdon, to the disintegration of his own family life and subsequent escape out of the depths of his Valley home's celebration of the Royal Wedding. Alex's life has been that of his Wales, from the heights of pure nationalism to the valleys which he equates with colonial acquiescence. Here we cannot avoid the suggestion that the mother - loved, despised, desired - stands for Wales and so the play becomes a complicated web of the personal and the political, where nationalism could be seen as a sublimation of his family problems. Alex's spiritual search for a self-identity cannot be disentangled from his search for a higher truth and for a form of nationalism where language is one factor. And as I suggested above, the political discourse could seem, in psychoanalytical terms, a case of transference: denying the real problem - the oedipal scenario where Alex nurses confused sexual feelings towards his mother and resents the intrusion and power of the (step)father - the hero interprets the triangular personal relationship as a political one. Consider nationalism as the metonym and it becomes an intriguing allegory. However we read *Marriage of Convenience,* Alex, like the other 'voices' here, is clearly experiencing an identity crisis, an individual separation from a culture that would give coherence to his sense of self.

Unlike Burton/Jenks, Ted John or Alex, Lee is not self-consciously Welsh. But Williams's critique of a homophobic Welsh culture here is a recurrent theme in his work, as is the position of social minorities in general. Lee seems to be happy with his gay identity, although less sure of his persona - he needs an extrovert

Matthew and an intelligent Carl to balance his own introverted self. But he can only create his own subjective identity in terms of external references (music, shops, TV, food) and a narrative that owes more to teenage romance than reality - in other words, his self-identity is a fiction constructed in a style imposed from without. He is oblivious to identity politics that would have allowed him to use his sexuality in a positive way, relying instead on superficial clichés. That isn't so very different from Ted John's world and is just as much a metaphor for Wales's reliance on myth and false image.

Frank Vickery is perhaps the most naturally Welsh of our five writers - he effortlessly captures the idioms and cultural practices of the South Wales Valleys - but is not really interested in issues of Welshness and avoids obvious political content in his plays. Yet is it more than coincidence that his 'voice', Eileen, is as fractured, alienated, confused, prone to selective memory and downright self-deceptive as any of our five characters? Her identity crisis is turned inward, however, as she has to choose between fantasy and self-destruction.

That crisis faced by each of our five 'voices' is presently also faced by the nation of which these five are all a part, a country in which they all live, a culture of which they are a part (and a very active part). Wales, at least to me as an outsider, has an identity crisis. To an extent it is the same problem discussed by Gwyn Alf Williams in the 1980s in his seminal *When Was Wales?* Today the crisis is more acute because Wales has something approaching semi-autonomy with a National Assembly and which is openly advocating a 'rebranding Wales' exercise and a collection of cultural institutions called the Welsh National Performing Arts Companies[19]. It is part of the United Kingdom and a country in its own right. Well, maybe ...

Wales's identity crisis is that faced by many postcolonial nations - in particular the European ones who have emerged from the shadow of an imperial neighbour. I would not presume to discuss that crisis here but simply state the obvious: that the cultural crisis of identity in Wales is exacerbated by the fact that it is partly autonomous, partly still run by Westminster; that there is not simply a Welsh/English language question but a multicultural one in a country where Hindi, Bengali, Gudjerati, Urdu and other non-European languages are also spoken; that there are apparently contradictory attractions in internationalism and independence; that employment roles have been rapidly changing; that inward investment from overseas-based multinationals sustain an economy that aspires to be self-sufficient; that internal regional boundaries have altered; that globally nationalism has become even more suspect; that macho masculinity rules culturally but women are powerful politically; and that previously potent symbols of Welshness have been shown to be inventions.[20]

If the promotion of national identity is a device which unifies through suppression of difference, then in a heterogeneous world Wales *must* have an identity crisis. Burton, Ted John, Alex, Lee and Eileen are all in personal identity crises which represent our common cultural crisis of identity, the crisis of postmodernism.

So: five examples of one man's voice, each struggling to create a fiction they can believe in, one that can make sense of their life enough to give them a sense of identity. But all five speak - metaphorically and literally - with a distinctive Welsh accent. They are, then, doubly fascinating as we wonder if we can ever identify who and what we are in the twenty-first century.

footnotes

1 'Signs of performance' have been known to practitioners for centuries: theatre space, words, textual delivery, facial expression, gesture, movement of the actors in the space and their proximity, make-up, costume, props, set, lighting, music, sound effects, and so on. They have been seized upon by modern theorists as a model of how semiotics (the study of signs) works, with its subdivision into icon, index and symbol - and hence by post-structuralists dealing in the terminology of 'signifiers' (the signs of performance) and 'signified' (what the signs stand for). Keir Elan's *Semiotics of Theatre and Drama* (Methuen 1980) is an example of the theory.

2 We could be tempted into scholarly forays into Lacanian psychology as well as post-structuralist theory; we will, you will be relieved to hear, generally avoid them.

3 Once we start discussing 'identity' we can get trapped in all sorts of semantic arguments. I simply wish to differentiate between 'reality', 'authenticity' and 'verisimilitude'. Steve Neale (*Questions of Genre*, *Screen* 1990) argues that while 'reality' is problematic and always constructed, 'verisimilitude' is what the dominant culture believes to be credible, a postmodern critical spin on the old idea of 'verisimilitude' as 'likeness to the truth'.

4 I personally would welcome Ian Rowlands adopting a 'Spalding Gray' approach to *Marriage of Convenience*, where he would not only direct (as he insists on doing) but *play* Alex. The resulting ambiguity about the relationship between author, actor and character would be intriguing. Spalding Gray is the American performer whose monodramatic performances are very psychoanalytical and raise questions about truth and

fiction (see his *Monster in a Box*, Vintage 1992).

5 See Katie Gramich's essay *Edward Thomas: Geography, Intertextuality and the Lost Mother* in *State of Play*, ed Hazel Walford Davies (Gomer 1998), where there are also six other essays on Thomas's work, including my own *Edward Thomas: Negotiating a Way Through Culture*. Thomas is far and away the most written-about playwright in Wales; for this reason, I may seem to have dealt with *Envy* in less detail than the other plays in this volume.

6 Monodramas often face such criticism - after all, they rarely have any action, often no sets, by definition no other characters on stage. However, since we are here examining them as the written word, in general the arguments can be left for another time.

7 It is a familiar analogy used by Rowlands elsewhere, particularly *Blue Heron in the Womb*, which is included, with my essay dealing with his political themes, in *A Trilogy of Appropriation* (Parthian Books 1999).

8 Phil Clarke at The Sherman Theatre has commissioned six Roger Williams scripts, including the Welsh-language POP for the theatre's youth company and several half-hour plays that were also broadcast on radio or television. Williams also wrote *Killing Kangaroos* for Made in Wales. The strengths of *Saturday Night Forever* were reinforced for me by conversations with Steve Fisher, director of the 1998 original and the 2001 Sherman productions.

9 The 'male gaze' is now a familiar concept in critical theory; the 'homosexual gaze ... decentres the aesthetic of the heterosexual male gaze' (Robert Wallace, *Towards a Politics of Gay Male Theatre*, quoted in Mark Fortier's *Theatre/Theory*, Routledge 1997).

10 These original productions were titled *Sleeping With Mickey Mouse*; the character's surname has had to be deleted for copyright reasons. Vickery's work has been unjustly neglected (totally, I believe) by academic critics because he is seen as too 'populist'. Indeed, his plays are extremely

popular with amateur companies. Partly because of this lack of regard, I spend disproportionately more space on *Sleeping With Mickey*. Sherman director Phil Clarke has championed Vickery and commissioned eleven scripts in the past ten years.

11 Disneyland is actually the original fantasy location in California, while Walt Disney World in Florida is the one most people know, although we tend to conflate the two enterprises. Eileen visits Disney World, and is also right on detail in terms of where she stayed, International Drive, near Sea World. See note 18.

12 All presented, of course, from her (woman's) perspective - psychologists might suggest, for example, that one reason so many men do walk out on their families after the birth of a child with disabilities might be because they feel ignored, as the mother pays more attention to the child's special needs.

13 For more on the binary theory of soap operas, soaps as women's genre and women's culture see Christine Geraghty's *Women and Soap Operas* (Polity Press 1991) and Christine Gledhill's *Genre and Gender: the case of soap opera* in *Representation*, ed Stuart Hall (Sage 1997).

14 This is a familiar technique used in a range of fictional biographies, from *The Diary of a Nobody* to more recent examples like *Adrian Mole* and Alan Bennett's *Talking Heads*.

15 The idea of the Other has become a crucial part of cultural theory, but it is also useful in this context. However, should we feel that discussion of identity has been appropriated by postmodern theorists, writers like Chris Norris (Professor of the history of ideas at the University of Wales, Cardiff) offer a welcome challenge to 'the fashionable rhetoric of 'otherness''. Unfortunately Norris is almost as abstruse as the postmodernists.

16 All fiction relies on the convention that we can talk about the characters as if they have their own existence when in fact they are created by their

authors; that fascinating ambiguity is emphasised by the monologue form. Further, what we have in this volume is a set of monodramas that does not constitute theatre (for that we would need a production, a venue, technicians, director and so on, and crucially an actor) but dramatic literature; we have two real-life subjects, author and reader (replacing the audience), mediated by a third fictional subject, the character - but, crucially, we lose the actor.

17 Turquoise eyes and dark or black skin do not generally go together, of course. But this is Eileen's fiction and could be evidence of her memory problem !

18 Here I might remind readers that Disney's fantasy universe, Disneyland and Disney World, the scene of Eileen's life-changing experience (however she might have reinvented it), is the subject for a study by the arch-documentor of postmodernism, Jean Baudrillard. In his *Simulacra and Simulations* (in *Selected Writings* ed Mark Poster, Polity 1988) he uses Disneyland as a model of his 'entangled orders of simulation'. Without wishing to get into the murky depths of postmodernist theory, we can say that part of Baudrillard's fascinating apocalyptic view of contemporary life is that we no longer have 'representation' of reality but a 'simulation'. He charts the successive phases of 'the image', from the reflection of a basic reality to the masking and perversion of a basic reality; to masking the absence of a basic reality; to bearing no relation whatsoever to a basic reality, the image becoming its own pure simulacrum. Disneyland and Disney World is not simply an imaginary land of pirates and astronauts, not even America in microcosm - more, it is, Baudrillard suggests, a 'third order simulation', there to conceal the fact it is real, indeed he argues that 'Disneyland is presented as imaginary in order to make us believe the rest is real'. Baudrillard's ideas rebut those of the American architect Robert Venturi, a pioneer of postmodernism (who felt that building development should be 'vernacular' and unplanned because that's what people were like) who affirmed that ' Disneyworld is nearer to what people want than what architects have ever given them. Disneyland is the symbolic American utopia.' French critic Louis Marin called Disneyland 'a degenerate utopia' ('an ideology realised in the form of a myth'). The

Italian philosopher Umberto Eco visited both Disneyland and Disney World, and other American 'cathedrals of iconic reassurance', in *Travels in Hyperreality* (Picador 1987). Ironically, Disney does not allow any description of Disney World (just as they did not allow Frank Vickery to use the full name Mickey Mouse in his title), so the 'actuality' remains hidden, controlled by Disney corporation's own version of it. Small wonder, we might think, that Eileen's notion of the real is challenged after a visit to this site of 'virtual reality' !

19 The project to 'rebrand' Wales may be a marketing exercise by politicians but is surely also a venture into hyperreality that extends the Disneyland-style sales pitch of the Welsh Tourist Board - and appropriates culture and the arts in its 'wales.com' vision.

20 In November 2000 a European survey was published that revealed how people outside the UK perceived 'nationality', described in terms of 'signifiers' or symbols: while Scotland was described in terms of kilts, haggis and scenery, Wales was signified by Diana, Princess of Wales, by Charles, Prince of Wales, and by the Royal Family in general ! Some public-relations work on 'branding' to do in Europe, to be sure !

Gareth Potter in *Marriage of Convenience*
photograph: Beth MacDonald